They Called my Husband
A Gangster

by

MRS. JIM (ALICE) VAUS

as told to

DOROTHY C. HASKIN

Contents

Alice Vaus and I became acquainted in the Big Tent in Los Angeles, shortly after Jim made his decision for Christ. Her happiness in the Lord and her delight at her husband's conversion were a joy to see. Again, I had the privilege of renewing my acquaintance with Alice Vaus when I was with Billy during his Hollywood campaign in 1951.

I am pleased that Alice has agreed to tell the story of her problems as the wife of a man who left the Lord out of his life. She had to hold fast to her faith that God would, in His own time, bring Jim Vaus to Himself.

Many women, across the country, have wanted her to write this story and I know all who read it will be blessed.

MRS. BILLY GRAHAM

CHAPTER ONE

Husband in the Headlines

The Big Year really was 1949. From January on, life began popping. Some of the things which happened did not seem important at the time but they grew larger and larger until my life cracked open like a watermelon which has lain too long in the sun.

Some of the things which troubled me were my husband, Jim Vaus, away from home all hours of the night. Or Jim talking about knowing Mickey Cohen and other so-called gangsters. Or Jim owning thousands of dollars worth of electronic equipment for which his business could not possibly pay. Or his buying furniture for our home that we reasonably couldn't be expected to afford.

Nor did I learn by questioning Jim about his activities. Not that he would not answer me, for he would. Far too glibly. Sometimes, as I found out later, he told the truth but it was so simple that I had not believed it. Other times, and this was far more often, he told me whatever he thought I ought to believe. It might be half truth and it might be wholly false.

Apprehension mounted within me, like distant drums coming nearer and nearer. Jim was becoming involved in something in which he should not be. More than that I would not permit, even to myself. How wrong or deep was the trouble I had only a vague idea. Bit by bit the story broke in the headlines. They screamed across the United States. I read them, alone in our home in Baldwin Park, California. To a young woman caring for not-quite-a-year-old Madeline, and carrying another child, the things the newspapers said about Jim were a shock. They called my husband a gangster!

When the events first burst into print, attention was mainly focused upon the fact that Jim had made a recording of a telephone conversation of Brenda Allen, later called "operator of Hollywood's most notorious house of ill fame" (*Hollywood Citizen-News*). She was alleged to have talked over the phone to Sergeant E. V. Jackson of the Los Angeles Police Department. The recording was supposed to prove that vice in Los Angeles operated under the protection of the police.

Jim had worked with the police department. After he received his discharge from the army, he went into the electronic business. He met Sergeant Charles F. Stoker, Sergeant Tom Dawson and Officer Riley of the vice squad and worked with them on several cases, including the Brenda Allen case.* His association with them led to his meeting Mickey Cohen, alleged gangster and consequently many of his racketeer friends. But now, the question in my mind was, was Jim still on the side of the police, or had he, somewhere along the line, changed sides?

Just to give you a general idea of what was being printed about my husband, in April, I idly picked up a copy of *Hollywood Nite Life*. It was supposed to be strictly a magazine of the entertainment world, telling where one should dine and who one could see and hear sing. This issue carried pictures of Lena Horne, singer, Liberace, pianist,

*See "Why I Quit Syndicated Crime."

Donald O'Connor, comedian and other entertainers. I flipped over the pages and there, in Jimmie Tarantino's column, I read:

WILL GRAND JURY INVESTIGATE BOWRON?

The Los Angeles Grand Jury can ask Mayor Fletcher T. Bowron many embarrassing questions regarding many shady deals with His Honor's Administrative Vice Department.

We have about twenty-five questions we would like answered. And so would the public. The puzzle involves Lieut. Rudy Wellpott and Sgt. Elmer V. Jackson.

Last week, we told you of the alleged "shakedown" between Lieutenant Wellpott and Mickey Cohen. We also pointed out that Lieutenant Wellpott and Mickey Cohen had been chummy at various public places.

Now, we would like Mayor Bowron to answer the following questions, of which we are certain he is capable of doing.

What does Jim Vauss, the "wire tapper" know about the intimate conversations which often took place between Sergeant Jackson and Brenda Allen, well known prostitute now serving sentence of 180 days?

What does Mayor Bowron know about Sergeant Stokes' connections with "wire-tapper" Jim Vauss? And what happened to the wire-recordings?

The article was much longer but I put the magazine down with a sick heart. The addition of the extra "s" to the spelling of Vaus did not change the fact that Tarantino was referring to my Jim.

Besides, there were the illuminating and inferring comments made by Florabel Muir in the *Mirror* on May 6:

SENDING HEAT BY WIRE

I hear that those wire recordings to be offered in the trial of Harold (Happy) Meltzer were sold to Mickey Cohen by the gent who made them for the Hollywood police vice squad.

They're supposed to be a conversation picked up between Brenda Allen and a cop.

Brenda, who was recently convicted on a charge of purveying

illicit love, was hotter than a depot stove because the protection she said she had been paying for wasn't forthcoming.

If the wire recordings get into the testimony a lot of other people are going to be hotter than Brenda was.

In the June 8th issue of the *Mirror* Miss Muir commented:

United States District Attorney James Carter says he's investigating the possibility that Federal telephones have been tapped and if he learns they have he'll take the matter up with the federal grand jury today.

Why does he have to wait for government phones to be tapped? It's just as much against the law to tap anybody's phone.

I've heard lots of citizens discussing the wire-tapping goings on recently and their reactions are interesting.

Some of them think it is okay for the police to tap wires to get evidence on suspected criminals.

But if you ask them how they'd like to have anyone listening in on their own private phone chats, that's an equine of a different shade.

The story of Sgt. Charles Stoker of LAPD is very interesting to me because it reveals the way of thinking that seems to be predominant among some young cops today.

They have lots of zeal, but not much know-how. Stoker says he heard that Brenda Allen was operating as a madame and the only way he knew how to get her was by listening in on her telephone calls.

So he asks a gent named Jimmy Vaus who just happened to be riding around in his car with him to put a bug on her phone.

He doesn't explain how he happened to be riding around with Jimmy (Sleight-of-Hand) Vaus.

Jimmy, who always seems to have been ready for any exigency, whips out his electronic tools and presto they're getting an earful of Brenda's talk with a Mr. Doe in the police department.

MR. DOE STILL RIDING HIGH

There followed a big to-do with the police brass and a member of the sheriff's vice squad setting up a trap in Barney Ruditsky's office in the Sunset Strip.

Several present at that session appear to have heard Mr. Doe and Brenda talking dough.

What I want to know is why only Brenda went to jail and why Mr. Doe continued to stay in the police department?

Detective Ronnie Harris, who made the pinch on Brenda and testified against her when she was tried, was dropped as a detective in the vice squad and put back in uniform and given a beat to pound.

Maybe Harris did something wrong, but his errors, if any, could scarcely have been worse than those committed by Mr. Doe, who has been identified as Sgt. E. V. Jackson.

Harris told me that Brenda threatened to have him broken and even if she wasn't successful the little prostitutes who hang around Hollywood think she did, so the effect is just the same.

This impression, of course, was given weight because Jackson continued on his merry way.

This is all very confusing to the public and has a tendency to cause distrust in their minds about the entire police department.

In a talk I had with Mayor Bowron before election he told me he was going to do something about the police vice squad and, brother, it's sure time he did.

I know I do not have to tell any woman how sick I felt when I read articles like those about my husband. People speak of their heart hurting but my entire body was one dull ache. Jim saw how unhappy I was but tried to ignore my feelings because, well, Jim was confident that he was not going to change. He expected to go on the way he was, bluffing his way through all the scandals and police investigations. He was young and going places. It seemed as if nothing anyone said or anything that happened could get beneath the surface of his "I'll get by" attitude toward life.

Our marriage of not even two years came close to the breaking point. Not that we argued, for we did not. Arguing always seemed so futile to me. You only expressed what you felt, added a few bitter words you did not mean and went on living the same old way.

But something, perhaps something we never had, died. After all it was I who had thought that marriage to Jim was a one-way ticket to happiness. Day by day living with him, with his indifferent treatment of me and his friendship with

[9]

people of shady reputation was dragging my girlhood dreams in the dust. Yet I dearly loved him. When he entered the room I seemed to come alive. When he was away from me, life was only a routine to live through until he returned.

The headlines kept popping. While they had started with the arrest of Brenda Allen, it was the Harry (Happy) Meltzer case which kept them boiling. Meltzer went on trial in May. The case is easiest explained by quoting an article which was printed in the *Los Angeles Times*. Sam Rummel was Meltzer's attorney. Of him the paper said:

OFFICERS ACCUSED

Rummel, in an opening statement to the jurors reiterated charges that Lt. Rudy Wellpott and Sgt. E. V. Jackson had attempted to obtain $5,000 from Cohen to be used in the campaign of Mayor Brown.

"We will prove through testimony that the two men first sought $20,000, then $10,000 and finally $5,000 from Cohen in return for their promise to quit harassing him," Rummel told the jurors.

"We also will show that Cohen told them he was a legitimate businessman and refused to be rousted further and charged that even if he gave the $5,000 he was sure none of it would ever reach Mayor Bowron."

NIGHT SPOT WITNESS

"We will further prove that Wellpott and Jackson took their lady friends on tours of such places as the House of Murphy, Slapsy Maxie's and other Hollywood night spots and told the management to 'send the check to Mickey Cohen.' We will have witnesses from each of these spots to so testify."

Mayor Bowron later issued a statement saying:

"I know nothing whatever of the facts. I never heard of the matter before, directly or indirectly. If there is anything at all to the statement made by Sammy Rummel, attorney for Mickey Cohen and his gang of hoodlums, I ask who is the accessory after the fact in not revealing the information to the District Attorney at the time of the happening rather than waiting until three weeks before the city election?

MAYOR'S COMMENT

"Assuredly, this will make clear in the public mind in whose corner

Mickey Cohen is and to what length he and his ilk will go in their effort to break into Los Angeles," the Mayor added. "This will provide another chapter for the State Crime Commission's report."

Police Officer Arthur Logue was the first witness called by Prosecutor William O. Russell.

Logue said he had been a member of the administrative vice squad for two and a half years and at approximately midnight January 15 in company with Lt. Wellpott and Sgt. Jackson, he drove to a spot across from Cohen's haberdashery in the 8800 block on Sunset Blvd.

After being joined by two other officers, Gene James and A. L. James, the quintet kept the place under observation for an hour and a half. At that time five men left in two Cadillacs. Logue said the five officers began trailing the first Cadillac, which contained Cohen, Meltzer and the driver Dave Ogul.

"We trailed it for nearly two miles," the officer declared. "We were in between the two Cadillacs and the rear Cadillac continually blew its horn in an apparent attempt to attract the attention of Cohen. They tried to pass us but we didn't let them."

Logue said they finally halted both Cadillacs at the intersection of Santa Monica Blvd., and Ogden Drive. He said he rushed to the rear right door of the first Cadillac, jerked it open and saw Meltzer sitting in the rear seat with a gun almost completely hidden in both hands.

DROPPED HIS GUN

"I started to raise my gun and then he dropped his gun and opened his hands. I reached in, picked up the gun, put it in my pocket and told Meltzer to get out of the car," Logue said.

Logue continued by saying he searched Meltzer and Cohen and then made a thorough inspection of the Cadillac. He then placed Meltzer in the police car and after other routine questioning the five officers drove off with the defendant.

These were the facts of the Meltzer case as reported by the press. Harry Meltzer was charged with "illegal possession of a gun." Naturally, Cohen wanted to help his friend out of a jam. With the idea of showing the arresting officers that there could be testimony against them and their connections with vice in Los Angeles, Cohen asked Jim to come to court with the much-discussed Allen recording.

[11]

On May fifth, Jim took some wire recordings to Judge Stanley Barnes' court. Of this the *Times* said:

The mysterious appearance of a second recording machine in the courtroom of Superior Judge Stanley Barnes yesterday touched off a wave of rumors that conversations of high police officials interested in the trial of one of Mickey Cohen's henchmen would be played for the jury.

Cohen himself escorted husky J. Arthur Vaus, sound expert, and the machine into the courtroom just as the first witness was called to testify at the trial of Harold Meltzer, ex-convict who is being tried on charges of possessing a deadly weapon.

After court hours, Jim came to my parents' home in Hollywood where Madeline and I were spending the day. We had dinner with my father, mother, sister Helen, and brother Bill. Shortly afterwards, outside, the dog barked frantically.

Jim and I ran out of the house but we were not quick enough to see who had disturbed the dog. Jim's car was parked in the driveway. He stalked over to it, saw that the glove compartment was open and everything was spilled out of it. He took one quick glance to check what was missing, then he jerked down the ceiling lining and ripped the upholstery off the seats.

"Jim, whatever are you doing?" I asked.

"You'll soon see," he answered as he yanked the floor mats out of the car. He strode back into the house and phoned the police, telling them that someone had broken into his car.

Within a few minutes, with sirens blowing, the police and press arrived. The police asked questions and the reporters took pictures. I stood around, hoping they wouldn't ask me many questions and they didn't.

The next day the *Mirror* printed a picture of Jim and the car with the caption:

APPARENT ATTEMPT TO DESTROY EVIDENCE

And the article about the "mystery raid" stated:

The raiders apparently were looking for the wire recordings Vaus yesterday took into Superior Judge Stanley Barnes' court where Meltzer is being tried for illegal possession of a gun. The wire recorder is said to hold conversations between Cohen and Los Angeles police officers. Cohen said the records "would blow the Meltzer case clear out of court."

Vaus said he usually carried the recording equipment in his car, but because of the "special circumstances" in this case he had left it in a safer place last night.

Maybe Jim had. I didn't know. What I wanted most to know was why he tried to make it appear to the police that the recordings had been stolen!

CHAPTER TWO

The Police Move In

Each day of the Meltzer case brought more headlines and hints about the secret recordings. On May 11, the *Mirror* ran the banner headline:

HOT RECORDINGS STIR PROBERS
NEW COP-COHEN JURY QUIZ LOOMS

Another headline was:

MELTZER CALLED "FORGOTTEN" AS RAP NEARS JURY

Indeed, Harry Meltzer did seem to be forgotten. Far more space in the press and more time at his trial was devoted to the alleged tie-in of the police department with the underworld. So confused was the case that when it went to the jury, the jurors were "hung." The trial had been such a mess of accusations and counter-accusations that the jury could not decide what was the truth any more than I could.

At least, the trial was over. I hoped with all the blind wifely love in my heart that this would be the end of Jim in the newspapers. All I wanted was Jim to settle down to the normal life of electronics engineer and family man. If only the police department and press would forget Jim and whatever recordings he had made!

But they were not to be forgotten. I understand that for several months there had been a grand jury investigation quietly going on. Now these activities began to gather momentum and take up space in the newspapers.

About that time, one evening, there came a mysterious phone call to our home. When Jim put down the receiver his face was ashen. I did not know at the time what the call was about and I am thankful that I didn't. I was worried enough and it would have terrified me. Someone had threatened bodily harm to Madeline and me.

I only thought of the call as more of Jim's carrying-ons. But the threat showed how agitated someone was over the recordings and it was responsible for our later, so-called, police protection. For my sake, Jim felt that he had to appeal to the police to guard us when actually he would have been better off if the detectives had not been in our home.

On Friday, June 3, Jim said, "Honey" in a casual tone. Sometimes when he spoke like that it meant nothing special. Other times it meant that once more life was going to jerk a rug out from under my feet. Cautiously I answered, "Yes."

"I'm going to Sam Rummel's office and take my wire recorder."

I nodded. But I didn't like his seeing Meltzer's attorney. It could only mean more of the merry-go-round mess.

"Leo H. Stanley, the chief investigator of the D.A.'s office is going to be there. He wants me to play some of my recordings for him."

"Oh." I never could get used to the fact that men from the District Attorney's office appeared to be chummy with men who, if they weren't crooks, certainly were close friends of crooks. To me, law-enforcers were one ilk and law-breakers were another. Yet, from what Jim told me, they seemed to be friends and working together. I still have not figured out some of the odd friendships.

"How about going to your mother's?"

"All right," I agreed. I didn't know whether to be pleased or not. As far as going to my parents' was concerned I enjoyed being there. It was pleasant to see my family. Too, when I was in Hollywood I was nearer to where Jim was and might see him sooner. But he had a habit of dropping me at my folks' home when he wasn't sure when he would be seeing me again. Maybe I couldn't figure out the whys and wherefores of Jim's business deals but my heart gave me a strange cunning when it came to our personal relationship. I sensed that he didn't relish this interview with Stanley and wasn't at all certain what would come from it.

I put on my new navy blue skirt and white linen jacket. I didn't wear a hat because Jim doesn't like women's hats. I packed a satchel of extra diapers for Madeline and followed Jim to the car. I always enjoyed riding with Jim. He drove as fast as the law allowed and a little faster but he was a smooth driver. He had the feel of a car, kept it in top-notch condition and it purred along the highway into Hollywood.

He dropped me at my parents' and after giving, what is to me, his little boy smile, he drove away. I stood at the window and watched his car disappear in the traffic. I prayed, "Dear God, please keep him safe. And somehow, someday, some way, lead him back to Yourself. You know Jim isn't all bad. It's just—" And because I loved him I didn't try to figure out why Jim was involved in a "vice probe." I didn't finish my prayer.

I busied myself, doing the things a wife does to try to keep from thinking. I fed Madeline. I drank a cup of coffee. With Mother, I discussed our family, our friends and if I thought my next baby would be a girl or a boy.

I watched the hands creep by on the clock. Each five minutes brought me closer to the time when Jim might return. What a way to wish away one's life! But that's the way it is when a girl loves a man who is in trouble. Time is something you have to live through. It is like creeping down a

Alice

long passage when you want to run. But you creep, knowing that if you keep going you will live through the long hours which keep you from your dear one.

Then, sooner than I had dared hope, Jim drove into the driveway and walked into the house. Had I been wrong in thinking he was apprehensive about his interview with Stanley? Events proved that I wasn't but meanwhile, he was back, bringing with him Lt. and Mrs. William Burns.

Mr. Burns was as typical a detective as I ever saw in a cartoon; tall, husky and wearing a felt hat with a slanting brim. His wife was a dark-haired, slender, pleasant woman. Jim nodded for me to follow him into the kitchen and he told me, "Honey, Mr. Stanley thinks we should have protection on account of the recordings. You remember that someone tried to steal them."

"Yes." I remembered too well that while some petty thief had broken into our car, it was really Jim who had wrecked it. What I did not know was that Jim had told Stanley about the threatening phone call of the previous evening and both of them had decided we should have police protection.

"Anyhow, this man Burns is to have dinner with us and spend the night at our house. We'll go out to dinner so you'd better leave Madeline with your mother."

"All right." Mother was a dear and always willing to take care of the baby. "But if we're going out, I have to have some new shoes to match my outfit."

We drove to Hollywood Blvd., where, in one of the smart shops, I bought navy sling pumps with white piping and a navy purse. Then we went to the House of Murphy's, where we all enjoyed the dinner. Jim is his genial best when a host. Burns acted as cocky as if he had a lien on the restaurant. Mrs. Burns was obviously impressed by the right hand column on the menu. And I was with Jim. That was enough for me.

Afterwards we drove to the Burns home to leave Mrs. Burns. Coyly, she insisted, "Dearest, you must go in first and see that everything is safe. And oh, you will lock up the house for me!"

He smirked, as if he were catering to a little girl. After he had assured her a dozen times that she was perfectly, perfectly safe, we started toward home.

On the way, Jim stopped at the Shaw's. I should say the Jenkins'. Odd, about Gwenn Jenkins' name. She was once the wife of Joe Shaw, brother of the former mayor of Los Angeles, Frank. She divorced Mr. Shaw and married Pete Jenkins, assistant city editor of the *Mirror* but nearly everyone referred to her as Mrs. Shaw. In the newspapers she was always called Mrs. Gwenn Shaw Jenkins, and her detective agency was known as "Shaw's."

Jim always claimed her agency was one of the best in town. He had done some work for her and this night he ran in to give a report to Mrs. Jenkins. The visit didn't seem important at the time, but all too many of these mole hills later became mountains.

Jim was there only a few minutes and then we drove home. Jim put the car in the garage and questioned, "I wonder if we'd better take the recording inside."

"They'll be safe tonight, don't you worry." Burns slapped him on the back. Jim gave one of his impassive looks, pulled down the garage door and we went into the house.

"I'll sleep on the divan," Burns decided, "then I can hear a noise from any direction."

"All right." I agreed and gave him a blanket. He took off his shoes and laid down. Jim and I went to bed. Right at that moment the Grand Jury, the wire-recordings, even a detective in the house, didn't seem important. Jim was home, where he belonged. There had been nights when he had not come home—when he had been busy! There had been times of sharp fear when I had doubted if he would come home. But tonight he was here and so I slept peacefully.

When I awoke, it was to hear Burns talking over the phone in a loud, excited voice. It was Saturday morning and I could tell—something new had been added.

I threw on my clothes and went into the dining room. Burns put down the phone, a woe-be-gone expression on his face.

"The recordings have been stolen," Jim explained.

"How? By whom?"

"We don't know. Burns and I went into the kitchen to make some coffee. I looked out of the window and noticed that the garage door was opened. I remembered I had closed it last night. Burns and I hurried out and sure enough, we could see where the trunk of the car had been pried open and the recordings were missing."

"I knew last night I should have brought those recordings in," Burns said dolefully. "The chief will never get over this. The press will ride him hard."

I could have reminded dear detective Burns that last night he had been equally certain he would hear any prowler. But he looked so miserable I could not bring myself to say it.

I went into the kitchen to make coffee. By the time it was ready to pour, the cars began to arrive and men poured out of them. Criminal investigators, with their scientific equipment, examined our car, searching for fingerprints. Detectives darted all over the place, pad and pencil in hand. Cameramen stood on the tops of cars, on hedges, shooting pictures. And the neighbors, whose friendships I had so carefully cultivated, peered out of windows or stood in their doorways, wondering what had struck the Vaus home.

By the end of two hours, every ash tray in the house was filled with cigarette butts and the kitchen linoleum was grimy from men tramping across it. But the police and press were gone. Without having found even a clue!

They left behind two detectives. The district attorney's office had assigned Chester C. Sharp and Aldo Corsini to protect Jim. Burns hadn't been able to. Perhaps two might. At least, they could keep each other awake.

Sharp and Corsini must have been made detectives because they looked like a million and a half other American men. Detectives, I understand, are supposed to look like the average man so they can be inconspicuous when following a suspect. Well, Sharp and Corsini were. They were both average height, heavily built and that day they wore light-colored suits and panama hats. Sharp wore rimless glasses but Corsini didn't. Sharp smoked cigars but Corsini didn't. To me, they looked like the fathers of some of my girl friends.

"The D.A. wants to talk to you about this," one of the men told Jim.

I didn't have time to tidy the house but changed into my navy and white outfit. Many times since I have been married to Jim I've been thankful that I wasn't the glamour girl type who took four hours to dress. All I needed was to run a comb through my hair, get into something tailored and have a moment to steady my nerves. Then, even if I were still agitated inside, I looked ready to follow Jim to the well-known end of the world.

Sharp and Corsini drove me to my parents' where I was dropped, as usual. Of course, it was good to be with Madeline and take care of her. Mother had to talk about everything that was in the newspapers. I explained as best I could what had happened.

"Why does Jim have to get into such a mix-up?" she lamented.

I wished I knew so I could have told her but I could only say, "Now, Mother, anything that Jim does is all right. You wait and see. It will come out all right in the end." I believed what I told her; only I did wish I knew exactly where my Jim was at the moment.

Later I learned that he, with Tweedledum and Tweedledee, and gone to Sam Rummel's office. Jim went into Rummel's private office to talk to Sam while the detectives waited outside. I suppose they must have been bored while they waited. They must be bored a great deal of time, waiting for people, for something to happen. When one gets close to a detective's life, it isn't too exciting.

Jim told Rummel the truth about the recordings. Rummel sneered and told him that neither the cops nor the gang would ever believe him. And that if the cops didn't give him a good working over, the gang would.

By now, Jim was definitely worried. When he got back to the car, he decided to tell Sharp and Corsini the truth. That is one characteristic I like about Jim. When he is cornered he always squares around and faces a situation. He did when, as a young student, he stole money from the Bible Institute. He did when he was arrested for holding up a man in Beverly Hills. He did so again when the army caught up with his pilfering. And that afternoon he admitted to Sharp and Corsini that no one had stolen the recordings the night before. Rather, he had got up early in the morning and hid them because Rummel and Stanley had been after him for days to play the recordings for them and he had reasons for not wanting to do so.

After they knew this, Sharp and Corsini became what Jim called "raid-happy." They were determined to have the honor of finding those recordings. They drove out to the house to look for them. Jim couldn't remember exactly where he had dug the hole for the recordings. He tried and tried but couldn't find the right spot.

The detectives decided he was bluffing again and that he had really hid them inside the house. They went in to look and nearly wrecked our home. They jerked the pillows off the divan and threw them on the floor. They overturned drawers. They took the canned goods off the shelves and dumped them in the center of the kitchen floor. They even searched through boxes in the bedroom closet and found Jim's army record.

Jim kept searching and finally paced off to where he had buried the recordings and dug them up. With glee the men piled into the car and drove as near fury as they dared in broad daylight to Jim's place of business. There, he had the equipment to play the recordings.

His business was called *Electronic Engineering—Consultants*. When the newspapers printed a picture of his shop the next day, they captioned it:

Front view of J. Arthur Vaus' electronic shop at 1025 N. Palm Avenue where district attorney investigators found $30,000 worth of equipment, including recording machines. Store is in the same building where Mickey Cohen maintains a haberdashery shop. It formerly was rented by Cohen, who was there last year when he narrowly escaped death in a gangland ambush.

Once inside the shop, Sharp and Corsini put the recordings on a wire recorder. How flat their faces must have fallen when it proved to be only an indistinct mumble of voices! Fooled once more! Were they angry and determined to find the right recordings!

They started to search the shop, and oh, the damage they caused. Jim said it made his heart sick to see them dump over boxes of small parts, condensers, resistors, tubes and everything in wild hodge podge on the floor. Some of the parts were so small they never could be sorted again. Some of the large stuff was so delicate that it was damaged beyond use. Little did the detectives care. Sharp and Corsini had but one objective to find the supposed Brenda Allen recordings. Anything in their way they tossed ruthlessly aside. When they were convinced that they were not there, they hustled Jim to the Hall of Justice, in downtown Los Angeles.

They went to the district attorney's office on the sixth floor, walking through a string of offices to one of the back rooms. Sharp and Corsini sat around, smoking, saying little. Jim sensed that they were waiting for someone. The silence, so far above the street, seemed to warn him that this quiet place had been chosen as a secluded place for trouble.

CHAPTER THREE

Jail Widow

In about a half an hour or so, Leo H. Stanley swaggered into the room in the district attorney's office where Jim, Sharp and Corsini were waiting. Stanley is a tall, thin, pale, brittle-looking man. He walked over to Jim and stood, his feet far apart, bracing himself, staring down at Jim.

"You smart *so and so,* I'll make you talk. I'll find out what happened to those recordings. You may push my men around but you'll learn you can't play smart with me and get away with it."

"I told your men the correct story," Jim insisted.

"You haven't begun to tell the story."

Stanley crossed to a table and deliberately pulled off his belt, his side arms, took his blackjack out of his pocket, removed his watch and rings, placing each item on the table. (This was so he would not leave a mark on Jim.) Then he pulled up a chair and sat so close to Jim that his left knee was between Jim's two knees. Tersely he asked, "Where are the recordings?"

"I don't know."

Slap came Stanley's palm on Jim's left cheek. "You do, too. You sold them to the highest bidder."

"I did not."

Swish came a slap from the other side.

On they went, blow after blow. I can hardly bear to write

about the beating. As long as it had to happen I am thankful that I didn't know about it at the time. I had often feared that some of the gangsters would harm him. But I had an inbred respect for the police and wasn't expecting them to hurt him. True, I had heard of the third degree but it never entered my mind that it would be used on my husband.

There I was, at my parents', holding Madeline in my arms, thinking Jim was safe because he was with Sharp and Corsini. Instead, the two of them were watching as Stanley hit Jim repeatedly with his open palm. And when slapping didn't make Jim talk, he hit him with his fists. (Jim's picture, taken the next morning, showed that his face had been bruised.)

Jim kept telling the truth but his face stung and he didn't have a moment's relief from pain. Sharp and Corsini began pounding him in the ribs. Jim says they really didn't hurt him much. The blows felt more as if the men were trying to please the boss by joining in, than if they wanted to hurt Jim.

Stanley kept demanding, "We know you stopped at Shaw's last night. That's where you sold the recordings, wasn't it?"

"No."

Slap.

"You sold the recordings to Shaw, didn't you?"

Slap.

The reason Stanley thought Jim had sold the recordings to Mrs. Shaw-Jenkins was because the information on the spools was supposed to be harmful to Fletcher Bowron's record as mayor. Mrs. Shaw, because of her former marriage to the ex-mayor's brother, was considered a political enemy of Bowron.

It must have taken all the self-control Jim possessed to sit there and take the beating. He was big enough to have mopped up the floor with all three of them but if Jim had ever struck back, that would have been all Stanley needed as an excuse to really work him over. And he would have had Sharp and Corsini as witnesses that Jim had hit him.

After what seemed like an hour of being slapped and punched, Jim's jaw snapped; dislocated. Tearing pains swept down the side of his neck.

"You did sell them to Shaw, didn't you?"

"Yes," Jim gasped. He was in such agony that he would have agreed to anything so Stanley would stop hitting him.

"It's about time." Stanley stood up and ordered, "Take him out to Shaw's and get those recordings. And one thing more, Jim Vaus, if you haven't told me the truth, the boys will bring you back here and we'll beat you until you can't lie down. I've had enough of your fooling around."

Jim managed to stagger after Sharp and Corsini, out to the car. They drove to Mrs. Jenkins' home and told her, "We want those recordings Vaus left with you last night."

Mrs. Jenkins' blue eyes narrowed. She gave the men one shrewd look and shrieked, "This is a frame up. Unless I see your search warrant you can't even look behind a door in this house. I'll get some protection. You don't dare touch me. I'll smear you and your smart office all over the front page."

She sat right down and phoned Virgil Pinkley, editor and publisher of the *Los Angeles Mirror* and her former husband, Joe Shaw, excitedly telling them the demands of the district attorney's office.

Sharp and Corsini saw they could get no place with Mrs. Jenkins. They warned, "This will go to the Grand Jury."

"Let it. Let it. You can't push me around."

Meanwhile, as the hours passed, I stared at that queer shaped instrument, the phone, wishing it would ring. When about ten-thirty, it actually did, I was so surprised that I jumped. Jim said, "Honey, I won't be home. I'm going to spend the night with the boys."

I sizzled. This was too much. Here I was, worrying about what had happened to him and he calmly phones that he is staying out all night with the boys. I muttered, "Fine thing."

"Honey, just wait. Everything will work out, if you'll be patient."

"I am patient, but—"

"You'll be hearing from me. Good night." He hung up. I had heard from Jim but it hadn't done me much good.

Unknown to me, "the boys" took Jim to the jail in the Los Angeles Hall of Justice and booked him on the charge of "Making a false theft report." (This was for saying the recordings had been stolen when they were not.) It was the strongest charge which they could frame.

I went to bed, in my old room. My teen-age sister, Helen and I had shared it for years. She had her own studio couch, a gift from one of our uncles. I slept in the double bed with Madeline. And I did sleep. One can stand being on edge only so long; then comes the relief of sleep.

In the morning I was feeling drowsy and comfortable when my brother Bill brought in the paper. He held it up so I could see the news.

My Jim was in jail!

I grabbed the paper from him and read every line about the case. Of course, all the main details were rehashed, the missing recordings, the theft at Baldwin Park, all I knew, plus some things I didn't know. But the awful thing was that my Jim had been arrested!

While I was still reading the phone rang. It was a friend

who wanted to be sure I had the paper. Yes, I had seen it but her call told me that so had all of my friends.

The phone rang again and this time it was an attorney friend of Jim's. He was a civil attorney who did not handle Jim's type of case but he promised to get another lawyer for Jim and to arrange for me to see Jim—tomorrow.

By this time I was anxious about the house and the dogs. I couldn't drive so Fritz and Margaret, friends of ours, drove me out. I was heart-sick when I saw the way the house had been wrecked. First, it was messy from the reporters and detectives tramping through it. Then Sharp and Corsini had tossed everything right and left regardless. I made a few half-hearted attempts to straighten up but saw that would be a week's work. I went out to the garage and then I had a new worry. Our car was missing.

Distressed, I went to a neighbor's and arranged for him to feed and provide water for the dogs. He looked at me kindly but questioningly. I told him nothing. Actually I knew nothing, except that my Jim was in jail and I was certain that he shouldn't be.

We drove back to Los Angeles, by the Civic Center. I glanced up at the Hall of Justice and for the first time I noticed that the windows of the upper floors were barred. I had walked by that building hundreds of times but never before had it occurred to me to glance up and realize that there was the jail.

And this long, hot Sunday my Jim was up there behind heavy steel doors. I felt as if I could tear out the bars with my bare hands and free Jim. But they hung limp at my side, for I was helpless. A frantic desire to call him froze on my lips for I knew he wouldn't hear me. Love that craves to help and yet is unable to is the most frustrated thing on earth. It is a mute, throbbing hurt.

I walked sadly around to the parking lot for the employees. On one side was a section for empounded cars. All by itself, stood our little car. It had been so unnecessary to go out to the house and get the car. But the police had done every mean trick they could. They wanted that recording. Jim couldn't or wouldn't give it to them, so they determined to hurt him in every way possible.

Fritz and Margaret started toward my parents' home and when we were almost there I saw a newsboy on a corner calling "Extra." Fatalistically I knew that an extra must be about Jim. I bought a paper and there was a picture of Jim in a blue denim jail suit. And in the article was an account of his arrest while in the army and of his imprisonment at the McNeil Island Federal Penitentiary. How black his record looked in print!

I could control myself no longer so I started to sob. My friends drove me home and for the first time my family knew that Jim had a police record. It was too much to face. Jim's married sister, Betty Wendt phoned but I couldn't talk to anyone. I lay on the bed and cried. Mother didn't say a word against Jim. She saw that I felt bad enough. Madeline gurgled but even her sweetness didn't cheer me.

Finally, my sobbing quieted enough so I could phone Betty. We discussed the mess and I realized, "I'll have to tell his father and mother. They won't have read the paper."

"I'll come by and drive you down."

I bathed my eyes and tidied up. Soon Betty arrived. She is one of the dearest sisters-in-law. She resembles Jim, is a brunette with blue eyes. But it is her disposition which wins friends. She is always quiet, ready to listen if you want to talk and equally content if you don't feel like talking. And she is always ready to help.

We drove to the Vaus home. They lived on a hill in a

residential district near downtown Los Angeles. The house was large, of frame, with a broad lawn and tall hedge in front. Inside, it was roomy and comfortable but simply furnished as could be expected of the home of a minister. Mr. Vaus had been a teacher at the Bible Institute of Los Angeles twenty-five years when he resigned.

When Betty and I went in, Mr. and Mrs. Vaus were eating dinner. They looked up, welcoming us. Mr. Vaus, with his silver grey hair, has the kindest, gentlest expression of any man I know. His wife is a dainty woman, who lives life with whole-hearted zeal, though her task be caring for her home, training her children or serving the Lord.

They looked so contented that it seemed wicked to disturb them. But they had to know about Jim and it would be kinder coming from me. I blurted out, "Jim's in jail, though I'm sure there's nothing to the charge but his record has come out in the paper."

Mr. Vaus stared at me in unbelief and then as if something within him broke, he bowed his head in grief. Mrs. Vaus threw up her small hands as if she had been struck, tottered to the couch and lay down. The blow was too heavy for her. Not much was said by anyone. We were all too grief stricken. How carefully they had tried to hush up Jim's past going astray, but it could not be hid!

Just as they were slightly recovering from the shock, in came his younger sister, Virginia. She is the one who resembles her mother. Besides, being pretty she has a gay manner. When I told her the news, she visibly wilted. None of us could think of anything to do to help matters, but somehow or other, God gave us the courage to go on.

Betty took me back to my parents' for the night. This time, I lay there, mostly staring into the darkness. I prayed little frantic prayers, please, God, please, straighten it all out.

The next morning Betty came in from San Fernando Valley again, and drove me downtown. With me, I took a white shirt, cuff links and a tie, as the lawyer had said to do. Jim had been wearing a sport shirt when arrested and he wanted a change to go into court.

Betty and I went into the Hall of Justice, into the office of the jail on the street floor and lined up with the others who wanted to visit a prisoner. Some of them looked as if they had just been released themselves. Others looked as if they had stood in line for years. There were young, brassy looking wives and mothers with the toil of years marked on their faces.

After I got the pass, we crowded onto the small elevator and went up. Some of the visitors got off at a floor where I could see relatives standing in front of a wire screen, yelling to the prisoners behind it. I shuddered. At least, I did not have to see my Jim in that noisy, cagelike place.

On an upper floor the guard took the shirt, examined it minutely and Betty and I took our place at the attorney's table. This is a table with a partition in the center, low enough so one can see a person's face over it, but high enough so one can't pass anything to a prisoner.

Betty and I watched the giant iron door. In a few minutes it swung open and out stepped Jim. His jaw had snapped back into place and he wore his broadest, most beaming smile. My heart sank. Wouldn't anything ever get Jim down?

I realize now that the smile was a big act for my benefit. He didn't want me to think any jail he was in was too awful. Actually, Jim loathed being in jail. There he was, in the heart of the city, able to see the busy traffic through iron-barred windows and yet he could not be a part of its throb. This was the greatest punishment that was ever imposed on Jim Vaus.

He assured me he would soon be "out." All he had to do was raise money for a lawyer and he would get Jim out on a writ. I didn't think of it at the time but it is odd that Jim raised the money from his respectable friends. His gangster friends, for whom he had risked his reputation and liberty, were deadly silent when Jim was in trouble.

Betty drove me back to my parents' home and there I sat, in a blue mood until Ralph Rubins, Jim's lawyer, phoned that Jim would be out and would get our car at five o'clock.

He did, for shortly after five a new world dawned for me. I had my Jim again. He picked up Madeline and me and we spent the night at Betty's. The next day we tried to pick up the pieces of our life. Due to the notoriety Jim lost several of his electronic accounts but in another way business boomed. He had a reputation, of sorts!

The criminal charge against him was dropped. It had been weak anyway. But that was not by any means the end of the brawl in the newspapers. There was the "Parade of witnesses in vice probe" when everyone even remotely connected with the case of the missing recordings was subpoenaed by the grand jury. There was the headline, VAUS SPILLS STORY OF VICE RECORDINGS. Vaus was such a convenient short name for a headline!

Sometimes I wondered how I, a girl who yearned for the quiet life, ever became involved in this noisy game of cops and robbers. How did I ever happen to marry Jim Vaus?

Jim

CHAPTER FOUR

Hollywood Romance

Hollywood is pretty much old shoe to me. I was born and grew up there. When you know where the cracks in the sidewalk are in a town, it ceases to be exciting. Hedda Hopper and Jimmie Fiddler, not withstanding, there are many side streets in Hollywood that are like those in any ordinary small town. There are plenty of frame houses, rose bushes and youngsters on tricycles.

I have known Jim Vaus since I was fifteen and began attending the First Presbyterian Church of Hollywood. I had ignored the high school department of my own age group and gone to the college department. It is one of the largest Christian college-age classes in the world, I am sure. The enrollment is over five hundred and most of the members attend each Sunday.

Probably the best known member is Colleen Townsend, the former motion picture starlet, who married Louis Evans, Jr., the son of the pastor. A couple of other well-known members are Connie Haynes, radio singer, and Lois Chartrand. In the same copy of the *Los Angeles Daily News* which published her picture and announcement of her signing a contract with Paramount Pictures, there was a story headed COHEN REFUSES TO SING BEFORE D.A.

The college class is taught by Dr. Henrietta C. Mears, a whole-hearted person who loves all young people. And some not so young. To know her is to love her. To hear her is to follow her teaching—unless, as I was, you are more interested in one of the young men in the class.

For even then my sin was putting Jim ahead of the Lord. I should have known better. Since I was a child I had loved the Lord and during my high school days I used to take my Bible to school to read during lunch hour. I knew the Lord Jesus Christ as Saviour but much Henrietta Mears said about living so close to the Lord that you know what He wants you to do and do it, well, there was a smoke screen between the Lord and me. It was Jim.

In my defense must be said that I did not realize that Jim was not a Christian. I did not know that he had travelled a rocky church road; his father's church, the Bible Institute of Los Angeles and others, until he came to "First Pres."

He knew all the words of religion as one can learn to repeat a sentence in a foreign language without understanding its meaning. He was welcome in any church because he had a friendly way with teen-agers, could make any party a success and lead singing. A young, undiscerning girl, such as I, could not see that he was not the Christian he professed to be. I took him strictly at the evaluation he placed upon himself.

At this time he was in the army stationed at March Field, moving up from Second Lieutenant to Captain. He often secured week-end passes, which he spent at his parents' home and at the church. At one of the Sunday evening services, Jim led the singing. My dad looked him over; then remarked, "That's the kind of a fellow you ought to get when you're old enough to marry."

I agreed with Dad completely. In order to become acquainted with Jim I began attending the Sunday evening servicemen's sing. Jim was usually there and after the meeting, he and his friend, Joel Allen, used to drive some of the girls home. Jim, with a grand manner, ushered the girls into either the back or front seat as he pleased. It took a little time before I worked up to the front seat but was I thrilled when I did! This was because it was Jim's custom to take whoever sat in front home last. It meant more delicious moments in his company.

My first heartache came when Jim became so interested in one of the girls at church that he no longer had time to take the gang home. She was pretty, popular and her father was one of the pillars of the church. Each night I prayed, "Dear Lord, please save Jim for me until I am a little older. You know I love him right now but he thinks I'm a kid. Please, Lord, make him wait."

My prayer was answered by Jim's suddenly stopping coming to church. I worried. What had happened? Then as unexpectedly, he came one Sunday night and after the meeting, he took me home alone. He told me, "Big things have been happening. The much ballyhooed wedding is off. I'm being transferred by the army and so, how would you like to write me from time to time?"

Would I? I wrote Jim nearly every day, sending my letters to an A.P.O. address. I received letters from Jim sent from Washington, D.C., San Francisco and other cities. He warned me not to give his address to any one. Often, in his letters he was mysterious about where he was stationed and what he was doing. I knew it must be something very important to the war effort. Sometimes he hinted that someday there was something he must tell me. I knew that whatever it was, must be thrilling.

In August 1946, Jim came marching home! I was teaching a Sunday-school class at First Presbyterian at the time. Jim attended the church a couple of Sundays and then suggested we visit some other churches. I did not even pray about it. Jim was first with me so I resigned my class to be free to go with him.

We visited around some but soon began attending the South Hollywood Presbyterian. A number of his friends from "First Pres" had transferred their membership because it was a smaller church. The Reverend Wilbur Antisdale was pastor. He was young, enthusiastic and we all enjoyed his vigorous sermons.

In those days, Jim enjoyed himself immensely being *the* busy man. He had an electronics shop on Century Boulevard, far from Los Angeles vice, Hollywood glitter or Beverly Hills swank. It was strictly an ordinary commercial business. Electronics had long fascinated Jim and he had studied them in the army so it was natural for him to go into that business.

It must have been around this time that Jim became involved with the vice squad of the Los Angeles Police Department. As far as I can remember, the first time I heard Jim mention his connections with them was one evening when we were with a couple of our church friends, Don and Annabelle Swan. Jim was telling Don about the way he, Sergeant Charles F. Stoker, Sergeant Tom Dawson and Officer Riley were trying to get "the goods" on Brenda Allen, who ran a house of ill fame. They had wire-tapped her phone and listened to her conversations.

"That sounds silly," I objected. "If she is guilty, why don't they arrest her?"

"Honey, you don't understand. Knowing a person is guilty and proving it are two different things. There is no use arresting anyone unless you can prove that he is guilty."

"Well, you don't need to be mixed up with such people." It embarrassed me to talk about such a woman. I didn't realize that even then vice and crime had become a part of Jim's daily life. Because I only heard him speak of those people occasionally they didn't seem real to me. Many a girl has drifted into a worse tangle on the current of love. To his friends, Jim Vaus might be only a swashbuckler but to me, he was Prince Charming. I loved every inch of his over six feet and every ounce of his nearly two hundred and eighty pounds.

During this summer of 1947, Jim and I were going steady. That part I liked. What I did not like was the fact that it looked as if we would still be going steady in 1957. When he had a date with me, he might keep it and again he might not. As it happened that certain Sunday in August when I learned that staring at a telephone wouldn't make it ring.

On Sunday Jim and I usually went to church together, to see some friends, drive to one of our favorite views in the Hollywood hills. Nothing spectacular but it was special to me, because it meant being with Jim.

This Sunday I looked for him from about one o'clock on. Maybe, I really didn't expect him until two because Jim wasn't the prompt type. My dream was always that he would be early because then we could be together longer but if only he came, I had to be satisfied.

I dressed in my summer suit and new tan blouse and waited. I stared at the phone. I gave myself a manicure. I stared at the squat black phone. I read all the short items in the *Reader's Digest*. I stared at the dumb, unresponsive phone. I tried combing my hair with a side part but went back to my usual off face pompadour.

Mother kept an eye on me all the time. Like most mothers she can cluck over her own so she grumbled, "Why you wait for that Jim Vaus is more than I can see. There are plenty of other fellows you could get, if you tried."

"I guess Alice can wait for him if she wants," defended

my fourteen year old sister, Helen. If ever anyone had an admiration committee of one, I had it in Helen.

I only answered, "Uh, huh." I stared at the phone and every number on the dial beckoned. All I had to do was dial his parents' number, hear his smooth voice and the suspense would be ended. He would have to give me some explanation. But by sheer force of will, I kept from phoning him. I couldn't help loving him, but I wouldn't let myself chase him. If only I waited long enough, surely he would arrive, full of reassuring explanations.

Each ten minutes that passed brought expectancy. I had lived that much longer and resisted the urge to phone him. Surely, soon he would recall our date and ring my number. No matter where he was, or what he was doing, he must remember me eventually. Six hours later, it was after seven and still Jim had neither come for me nor phoned.

My resolution broke into a thousand brittle bits. I had to know what was wrong. Something desperate could have happened to him. I dialed the six numbers that should either bring me Jim's mellow voice or news of his whereabouts.

"Hello."

His sister Virginia had answered. Distressed to the point of admitting I had been "stood up" I explained, "This is Alice. I've been waiting for Jim."

"Isn't he with you? That's where he told us he was going."

"No, he isn't," I answered, feeling even worse than I had. Until now I had been presuming I would reach Jim at his home but that hope had proved to be a blank.

"Listen, Alice, don't sit around all your life waiting for Jim. Let's you and I go out together and show him you can have a good time without him."

"All right," I gulped. Virginia was right. I should show

[38]

Jim that I didn't care if he came or not. Let him come by the house later and find I had gone out without him. And in my heart I hoped, he'll miss me. If only he misses me enough, next time, he will keep our date.

So Virginia and I went out together and I went through the motions of a young girl enjoying herself. From sheer nervousness I laughed at anything that resembled a joke. And resolutely I promised myself, I am going to get over caring the way I do for Jim. What if his front wave does have a teasing way of falling down his forehead, he is irresponsible and impossible. Mother is right. I can find someone else and I had better look around while I am young enough. I'm not going to spend my life waiting for him— or am I?

I went home with Virginia to spend the night. I always enjoyed being with the Vaus family and they approved of my going around with Jim. They were a fine, upright family and I based much of my confidence in the fact that Jim had grown up in this home. At church I had heard many a whisper of Jim's fickleness, of his extravagance, of his egotism, but I shook my head at these accusations. Jim had been raised in a Christian home and therefore he was all I could expect a man to be. The fact that he broke dates with me did not prove that he was doing anything wrong. Rather, I felt the reason he broke them was because he did not care enough for me.

That night I slept in one of the large upstairs guest rooms. At least, I lay quiet but in reality I was very much awake. I strained to hear the creak of the downstairs door opening, or the pad of Jim's footsteps on the stairs. I wanted to hear him come home so I would know he wasn't lying by some deserted roadside, hurt and alone. But I couldn't stay awake long enough. Sometime in the dark hours I drifted off to sleep and did not hear Jim come in at four.

It was a custom for the Vaus family to eat breakfast together. This morning, however, Mrs. Vaus could not come to the table because she was ill. Virginia and I sat down and after his father called him repeatedly, Jim joined us.

I would not look directly at him. I would not let myself. He had an impish way of smiling and if he caught my eye and I forgave him, I would have all of yesterday's heartache to live through again.

I was not the only one who was fed up with Jim's behavior. Virginia was not speaking to him either. Anything we had to say was relayed through Mr. Vaus. Virginia and I felt that Jim must learn that we loved him too much for him to be gone hours without a word and, human like, we showed our love by our scolding attitude.

When breakfast was finished, Jim stepped directly in front of me and suggested, "You better let me drive you to work. You'll be late if you don't."

I glanced at the clock on the mantle. He was right, it was getting late. Besides, on the way, I could have it out about yesterday. I'd tell him, oh, so very calmly, but definitely, that he must not neglect me like that again. He must make up his mind to a formal engagement and marriage. Or—I wouldn't permit myself to think of an "or else."

At that time I was working for "Protan," who manufactured a product which was an aid in reducing. I had gone to work in the office when I was still attending Hollywood high school and when I graduated, began working full time. The office was on Hollywood Boulevard, across from Grauman's Chinese Theatre. That is at the far end of the Boulevard, beyond Highland Avenue. There was a time when to say "The Boulevard" meant only from Vine Street to Highland, a distance of about twelve blocks. All the smart shops were located there. But Hollywood's glamour spread and the Chinese Theatre, one of the *must* tourist stops, was built beyond Highland.

This morning Jim drove out Sunset Boulevard to Hollywood. With each mile I asked, "Jim, exactly when and if are we going to be married?"

"Honey, you know we'll be married some day. It's only that I think I ought to have a thousand dollars saved before I marry. That's sensible, isn't it?"

"Too sensible! It doesn't sound like you. It sounds like a license for drifting. Jim, here we are, supposed to be engaged and who knows it? Who? Even your family and mine only guess that we are."

"Honey, it's only that I thought we ought to get a little closer to the actual event before we spread the news around."

"But Jim, we're getting closer to nowhere. I sit around and wait and nothing happens. On and on we drift."

"It will all be all right some day."

"Some day—" I stared through the windshield and the traffic blurred before my eyes. Some day can seem so far off when one is eighteen and in love. But Jim wasn't to be moved. I shook back my tears.

Jim parked, and then, what good had it been for him to get me to work on time? For fully half an hour I leaned against the fender, insisting that he make some decision. It wasn't that I was stubborn, but that I was heartsick. In a low, desperate tone I kept repeating, "But Jim, I don't want to drift like this. What do we gain?"

"But Honey, don't you see—" was all he would say. Finally I realized that I not only wasn't getting any place but that I was not going to, so I went inside. How low can a romance get!

Chapter Five

Wedding of High Hope

In the Protan office, between typing orders, I complained to the other girls of the way Jim had treated me the day before. One of them said, "Why don't you give him the air? A guy like him can string a girl along for years, and believe me, I do mean years."

But Elsie, the newest girl in the office, said, "It's your business, but if it were me and I loved a fellow, well, I'd love him anyway."

I turned my face away quickly to hide my emotion because she was too right.

The day passed and Jim did not phone. He could have. He had plenty of other times. If he had wanted to talk to me he would have, quickly enough. But apparently he had nothing further to say. I was so confused that I hurt deep inside; to drift indefinitely seemed beyond my endurance.

When I left the office I could only hope that I had filed the orders correctly. I had not been a very valuable employee that day. At home, after dinner, I settled down on the divan to spend the evening with an interesting book. I was far behind on my reading and thought I might as well cultivate a liking for books. I could see that as long as I continued dating Jim Vaus I was going to have spare time to read.

Ding-a-ling, ding-a-ling went the phone. I frowned at it. It wouldn't ring yesterday when I wanted it to but now, when I was resigned to waiting, away it went, ding-a-ling. I picked up the receiver and casually answered, "Hello."

"Hi, Honey, when do you want to get married?"

"Let's not go into that," I instinctively protested. I didn't want a big build-up for an even bigger letdown.

"But Honey, it is what I want to go into. I'm coming right over."

He hung up. I warned myself that he might be, and probably was, kidding. Just a bright idea of his. But I was careful to comb my hair.

Within fifteen minutes he walked into the house; which considering he had come ten miles in heavy traffic was far too quick. He sat down and began, "Honey, when do you want to get married?"

I studied him. My Jim, the twinkle in his blue eyes, the weighed way he had of speaking, his hands so dexterous; I wanted nothing else but to spend my life with him. Beginning as of that moment. Yet fearful he might not be in earnest, I cautiously asked, "Jim, what made you change your mind?"

"I don't know. I just decided I had fooled around long enough."

Jim is like that. I had seen that trait in him before and I was to see it again. He would drive me frantic with his devices and then, suddenly, when he was ready to do right, he was ready to go all the way. A glow swept through me and I suggested, "How about October? On my birthday?"

"Suits me."

So that was it! We went for a drive and made many, many a plan. We talked of such important things as where we would live, where we would be married and who would perform the ceremony. I suppose, in a way, that was the happiest evening I ever spent. All the gossamer dreams of my girlhood were given life.

The hour grew late. He drove me home and as I was getting out of the car I remembered yesterday. I asked, "Oh, Jim, where were you yesterday?"

"With the vice squad," he replied curtly.

"Oh." I kissed him good-by and as I walked into the house I thought, Jim's being with the vice squad must be pretty important. As far as I knew then anything connected with the police department must be all right.

For the next couple of months my heart whispered, "The date is set, the date is set." All day long it murmured, "You're going to marry Jim. You're going to marry Jim."

I planned for my wedding with Jim to be the most perfect possible. I dreamed and schemed to have the most beautiful wedding gown in Los Angeles. Every visit to his family was full of talk of guests, ushers and decorations. The wedding was to be held at the church of Betty's husband, the Reverend Lester Wendt, in Canoga Park. My parents also threw themselves whole-heartedly into our plans, even to the detail of buying a guest book for the wedding. My life revolved around my coming marriage.

Even as my heart rested in the warmth of his love, the warnings began. Not from either family but there were church friends who were not convinced of Jim's sincerity and felt it their Christian duty to warn me before it was too late. I brushed their words of caution to one side. And then came an even stronger warning; from Jim, himself. One day in September, when I was at work, Jim phoned, saying he had something important to tell me.

I was curious to know what it was. That night we went for a drive to our special spot high in the Hollywood hills. He parked so we could see over the city. The long string of lights was Vermont Avenue, one of the longest streets in the world stretching from the mountains to the ocean. It was quiet and still above the traffic of the city, and high in the sky where the bright, radiant stars.

"Honey, remember when I was in the army I used to write you that I had something to tell you sometime?"

"Yes," I recalled and thought, I am going to learn Jim's exciting secret; perhaps the wonderful things he did in the army. I twisted around so I could look straight in his face. He was pale and tense. I had never seen Jim so upset before and I sensed that what he was going to tell me was even more serious than I had anticipated.

"Honey, I must tell you. It happened when I was going to 'First Pres.' It was a big mess. Remember when I was at March Field—" He paused as if groping for the right words.

I nodded, encouraging him to go on. More than anything I wanted him to finish so he would get over being nervous. I was more concerned about the way he felt than hearing his news.

"I was in a position to get hold of priorities, and well, I got some for my friends and for myself. Besides, there was so much war-time waste and equipment around loose that I acquired an army projector to which I had no right. Being war time 'misuse of government priorities and misappropriation of government property' was a serious offense. I was sentenced to ten years in prison."

"Oh, no, Jim!" Instinctively I put my hand on his, not thinking of what he had done, but of the awful idea of his spending ten years in prison.

"I'll never forget that awful moment. The very room spun. Fortunately for me, my case automatically had to be

[45]

reviewed by President Roosevelt and he remitted my sentence to five years."

By that time I was able to count and figured, "But, Jim, you weren't gone five years."

"No, at the end of five or six months my case was reviewed again. But this time the war-time fever had subsided; so I was pardoned and ordered to Fort Leavenworth for a period of rehabilitation. Then, after the war, because of my interest in electronics, I was assigned to a group of officers who toured the country, speaking in colleges."

"Oh." All I could think was that my Jim had suffered out of proportion to what he had done.

"You do forgive me, don't you, Alice?"

I glanced at him with surprise. Why, there was nothing to forgive. He was my Jim who could do no wrong. I edged toward him. He took me into his arms and kissed me. And what girl is interested in a man's past at a time like that?

Only once more that evening did I give the matter another thought. I asked, "But if you were in prison how could you mail me letters from so many places?"

"I gave them to fellows who were going out." He tilted his head, smiling in his sly way. He was just too smart!

So, in a general way, I knew all there was to know about the past of Jim Vaus when I married him. I knew he had been in prison. I knew he was working on unsavory cases with the vice squad. But more important, I knew that I loved him.

On October 23, 1947, we were married at Christ Community Church in an especially beautiful and sacred ceremony. Both his father and brother-in-law officiated. We had a double ring ceremony with Jim giving me a thick gold band, because that was the type of ring I wanted. I had the wedding dress I had dreamed of; white satin long sleeves, sweetheart neck, and long veil. The bouquet Jim gave me was priceless. There were two large white orchids in the center, surrounded by gardenias and four dozen lilies of the valley.

We had rented a home in North Hollywood and spent a couple of days there before we started on our honeymoon. Jim had a "break" as far as the honeymoon was concerned. He had been called to Washington to demonstrate some of his electronic equipment for the F.B.I. Jim had perfected some interesting equipment. For instance, he could draw sound through solid walls. Or sit at a listening post several miles away and hear what was said in a given room. Or he could drive several miles behind a car the police wanted to trail and with an electronic devise, follow it.

I suppose, as I look back, Jim treated me rather casually on our honeymoon. He was pretty much interested in Jim and what Jim was doing. But I had married the man I wanted and I was happy, even if much of my happiness was but a reflection of my own love for Jim.

All too soon, the honeymoon was over, and we settled down in North Hollywood. But from the very beginning, my happiness was spoiled by Jim's connection with the vice squad. Often, he was away from home all night long. When I questioned him about where he had been, he could always tell a plausible story. I intensely disliked his being entangled in cases with such questionable women as Brenda Allen and her ilk. Too, I learned that some of the police were too friendly with these women. They were a bad influence for my Jim. I grew to dread his kissing me lightly and saying, "I'll be with Dawson."

When he did, I knew that long, dull, groping hours would pass without my hearing a word from him. I used to sleep late and do my housework at night, anything to pass away the time. The dark shadows crept across the window and I was alone. Sparkie, my golden cocker spaniel, was my only comfort. I was married to the man I loved; to a man who did not walk with God.

Within three months of the wedding I was hoping and planning to find a way to get Jim away from his associates. I wanted to move some place where he would spend more time with me.

As long as we lived in North Hollywood, we realized just over Cahuenga Pass was Hollywood with its lax morals and easy divorce. Not that there aren't plenty of average, respectable citizens in Hollywood. There are. Carpenters, waitresses, doctors, bankers and such. Like my folks. Plus the Hollywood Christian Business Men's Committee and a number of well-attended churches.

But undue newspaper publicity has attracted to Hollywood both the best in talent and the lowest in morals. There one finds men and women from every corner of the world seeking success in the motion pictures. Also, one finds leeches who exploit human weakness and make money a modern golden calf.

I wanted to get Jim, with his naturally ambitious nature, away from this city where too many sought to get rich by quick and unethical methods. I loved him, had faith in him but my intuition told me that he and I would be happier away from even the law's side of vice.

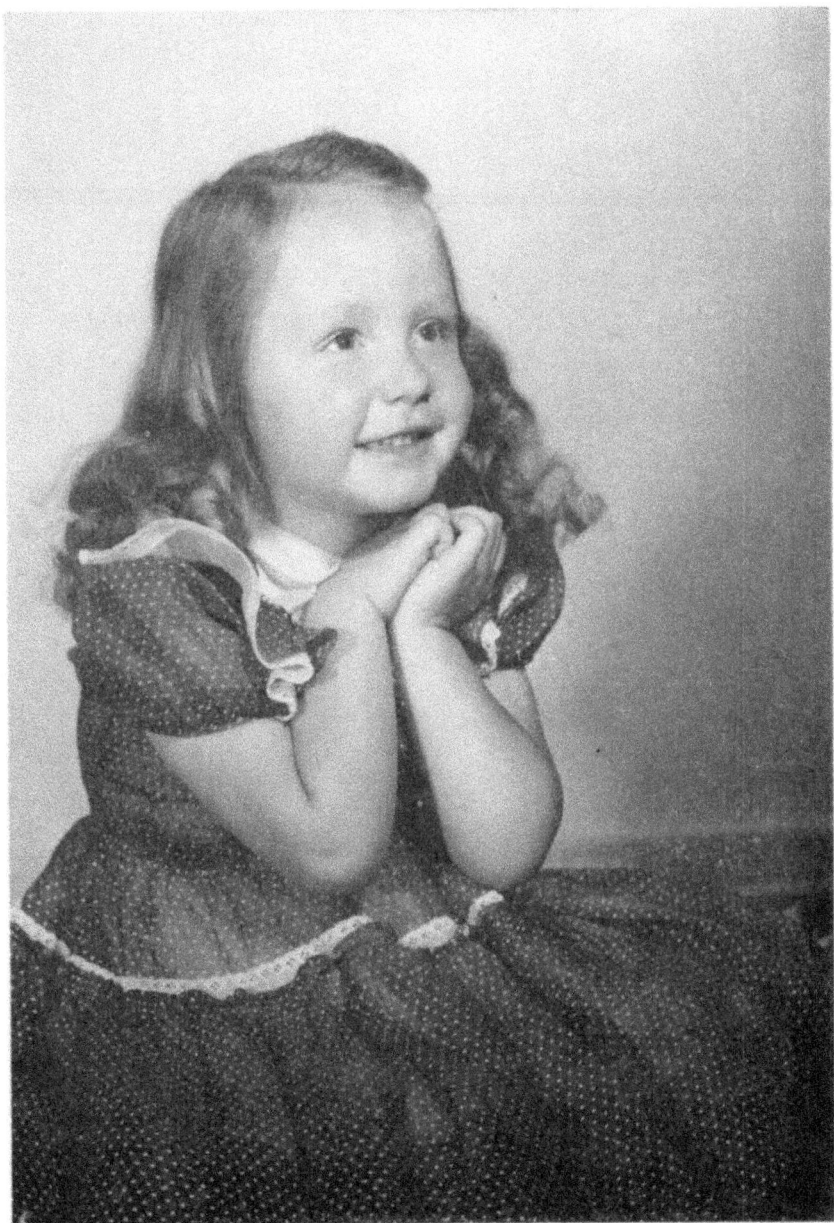

Madeline Louise

CHAPTER SIX

Ways to Keep a Husband

The way to move Jim seemed obvious. The rent we were paying was far too high, and the house was too small. The home of Jim's childhood had been roomy and he moved around our honeymoon bungalow as if it were built for a pigmy. I opened my campaign with "Jim, as long as we're sinking this much money into rent, why don't we buy a place of our own?"

"We'll look around," he smiled at the idea. Of course, owning his own home appealed to Jim. Owning anything appealed to Jim in those days.

When we studied the ads in the newspapers, I favored those which were in one of the small towns surrounding Los Angeles. One was for a home in Baldwin Park, on the way to Riverside, about twenty-five miles from the Civic Center of Los Angeles. This seemed about as far from Hollywood as I dare hope to move him.

I followed Jim out of the house, into the car with a happy song in my heart. This was going to be our place, for sure. We located the house, a rambling, ranch style home on a half acre of ground. Then we had to look up Mr. F. B. Johnson, a tall, lanky built man, kindly but smart.

He sized us up to see if he thought we really could afford the house. Jim sized him up to see how much of a line it would take to convince him that we could. As often as

Johnson gave him an opening, Jim picked it up, letting it be known that he was a big shot in electronics. Ever so casually he mentioned the names of some of his best known accounts. When they finished bargaining, the down payment was reasonable but oh, the monthly payments were stiff!

By April, we had moved to Baldwin Park and I was certain I was going to have a baby. Jim was delighted. From the very beginning we planned to have four children. And so, everything was set for Jim to stay home—a house in the country and an expecting wife.

Only, life did not turn out that way. Not with Jim. Things just don't. Instead he had me planted in the tules and I was more lonesome than ever. We had very little furniture, only what was necessary in the kitchen and a couch on which to sleep in the living room. This emptiness made the house seem even more lonesome.

We lived at the end of a dead-end street. I used to stand at the huge window in the living room and hope and pray that Jim would come home. Sometimes it seemed as if the strength of my desire for him would draw him. Surely if there were such a thing as human magnetism my longing would have pulled him.

But my love was not the power needed to keep Jim on the road of being a law-abiding citizen and happy family man. The love of no wife is strong enough to change a man. I could not pull him one inch beyond which he was willing to go.

When he was home, he was impatient with our bare rooms. Often, he would stride around and declare, "As soon as I get my business on its feet, we'll fix this place up. Get modern furniture. A deep freeze. Save you going to the store. An electric stove. A television set. I want a home that looks like something."

"If only we had a bed I'd be happy," I countered with my less expensive but more practical suggestion.

"Look at the hours I put in with the vice squad and what good does it do me? The officials are always harping budget, budget, budget. No wonder Los Angeles is riddled with vice and crime. If Mr. John Citizen won't pay for cleaning up his city, he'll have to expect the crooks to run it. Everything in this world costs, including good government."

I enjoyed hearing Jim talk. He always sounded important to me when he strode around the room sounding off on government.

"My trouble is, I'm on the wrong side of the racket, the small money side."

I listened with less happiness. I didn't like Jim seeing so clearly that the crooked side had the money.

"All I ask is enough money to have a properly furnished home, a good car, the things a man needs in this world. Just enough to content me."

I wondered then if it would be ever possible to satisfy Jim. I had the feeling that trying to do so would be like pouring water in a barrel with holes in it. Always there would be something more that he wanted.

I didn't say those things to Jim. Instead, I tried what is called woman's guile. I would make him over into a family man by having him replant the garden. The former owner had the large backyard planted with vegetables. With vigor, Jim cleared it off, put in flowers, grass and a sprinkler system.

Odd, how a wife can try to make over a man and unless God has moved upon the man's heart, she defeats her own plans! The garden was not the bright idea I had hoped it would be because it took the time we should have given to God. We had been attending South Hollywood "Pres" more or less regularly. Jim had sponsored a high school group.

But he had lost his taste for church and the yard became an increasingly used excuse to "stay home and get a little work done."

I didn't like that. I knew our place on Sunday was in church. When I urged Jim it was like trying to make an impression on a balloon. You can hold it down for a second but lift your finger and it bounces right back to its own size and shape. Naturally, the instinct of a woman when she sees her husband drifting, is to force him back on the right road. But Jim wouldn't be forced. Probably no man can be.

When he was away I read my Bible a great deal, searching for guidance. I found it. It wasn't easy to follow. It promised to be a long hard road to travel, one of patience and forbearance, but there it was:

"Likewise, ye wives, be in subjection to your own husbands; that, if any obey not the word, they also may without the word be won by the conversation of the wives" (I Pet. 3:1). In the revised version, the verse reads, "Be gained by the behavior of the wives."

This was the verse I tried to follow and on which I based my hopes that some day my marriage to Jim would be all it should be. I did not demand, insist, or plead with Jim. I only prayed and waited, even when the situation seemed to go from bad to worse.

I remember the first time he came home and said, "Honey, who do you think I met today? Mickey Cohen."

I didn't answer. I was trying to think and I wasn't going to tell Jim that his big news wasn't too exciting because I had to think twice to recall who Mickey Cohen was. When I read the papers I gave one quick glance at the headlines, a run down of the latest murder and a study of the department store ads.

I have mentioned Cohen several times before but because

I feel there are others to whom the name of Mickey Cohen doesn't mean as much as that of Billy Graham, I'm going to explain more fully who he was. At least, who the police and press say he was.

According to some of the national magazines, he was "the undisputed boss of Los Angeles gangdom" (*Time*, 1949). He was supposed to head up gambling joints in and around Los Angeles. The extent to which the stories told about him were true, I don't know. Some say that crime is syndicated in the United States and that Cohen was tied in with the biggest gamblers in the country. Others insist that organized crime in each city is a private affair; that there is no national connections other than because they are in the same business one gambler might borrow money from another.

Be that as it may, gambling is illegal in Los Angeles but plenty of it goes on. There are many swanky gambling houses, raided occasionally but always thriving. It was alleged that at the head of them was Mickey Cohen. The gamblers paid him to protect them from each other and he paid the police so the gamblers were not out of business.

None of these allegations against him were proven though the police and the press harassed him for years. He was arrested when the federal government indicted him for income tax evasion. He was tried, convicted of evading $156,000 income taxes, sentenced to five years imprisonment and fined $10,000.

The most unsavory messes he was in were the shooting escapades. When he shot Maxie Shanman, Cohen was questioned by the police but he convinced them he shot in self-defense. Later, "Hooky" Rothman was shot in Cohen's haberdashery while Mickey was in the washroom washing his hands. Another time when Cohen and some friends left

Sherry's, a nightclub on Sunset Boulevard, they walked into a fusillade of bullets. Neddie Herbert, Cohen's right hand man, was killed. Cohen, Dee David, a girl with the party, and Cooper, a plain clothesman from the State Attorney General's office, were wounded.

This was the man my husband had told me he had met. He continued, "Harry Grossman of Ruditsky's Detective Agency said if I'd go to Cohen's haberdashery, he thought I could pick up some money."

"Haberdashery?"

"Sure, he's in the same business as Truman used to be. Does Cohen have a swanky place! Indirect lighting. Walnut paneling. Takes some money to have a store like that! You know what he wanted? He asked me if I ever 'bugged' his house for the police department."

"And had you?" I asked, trying to sound casual but hoping to learn a little something of his operations with the vice squad.

"Not little me. Anyway, I went out to Cohen's place and found the bug."

"How?" I asked. Many of the things which Jim did with electronics were too involved for me.

"I've a high-frequency transmitter and receiver which sends signals into the ground and returns signals if any metal object is picked up, and a highly sensitive meter which computes the depth at which a metal object is buried. Within ten or fifteen minutes after I arrived at Cohen's place, I found that the 'bug' was concealed in a section of a built-in wood-box. I got rid of it for him, and by the way what do you want the most for the house? I picked up a few bucks doing the job and I don't mean too few."

Jim's not too few bucks held no charms for me. I did not like Jim doing business with a man with a reputation such as Cohen had. I warned, "You'd better stay away from that man."

"Don't you worry about me. Anything I do for Cohen will be legal. Why, the police had no right to 'bug' his place. I'm more within the law taking out the microphone than they were putting it in."

As far as I was concerned, the matter drifted. I had something more important about which to think. It was getting close to November and within me stirred a young life. On the twelfth, I was standing in the kitchen when suddenly I felt a searing pain. I knew—this is it!

We had no phone so I went down to a neighbor's to call Jim. I told him, "In a couple of hours or so, you'd better come home and take me to the hospital."

"I'll be right home."

I hung up the receiver with a wry smile. This was one way to get Jim home. Too bad I couldn't have a baby more often.

I wanted to leave everything about the house as neat as possible so when I went home I began raking the leaves in the front yard. Suddenly I heard a siren. I whirled around, and saw—heading straight down our dead-end street, an ambulance. I knew—it was that crazy Jim Vaus. He couldn't take my having a baby calmly. Yet I knew the baby might not arrive for hours. I hurried inside the house, my face scarlet. I was not going to the hospital in that contraption.

But I did. I not only rode in the ambulance but I had to lie down with the attendant timing my pains and Jim hovering over me. It was about five o'clock and we went through all the down town traffic. I could see out the window, at the crowds on the sidewalk staring at me.

When I arrived at the *Queen of Angels Hospital* in such style, the staff knew I would have my baby any second. But

[55]

I didn't. It was not until the next morning that the dear, Madeline Louise arrived.

How precious she was! But I wonder if I would have been quite so blissful if I had known Mickey Cohen was paying my hospital bills.

Jim's relationship with Cohen had grown steadily closer. He had installed an electronic warning system around his house. He moved his business into the same building as Cohen's store. He told the police department that he was "too busy" to go on cases with them.

All I knew was an occasional mention of Cohen's name and the sudden opulence in our home. This, of course, could have come from Jim's business. He had always talked of the day when "things began clicking." He did have several well-paying accounts, such as J. Paul Getty. Jim did a great deal of work for him and often drove his Lincoln Continental.

I happily accepted the new furniture, the better equipment in the kitchen. Yes, and the barbecue in the back yard, where on Saturday nights, we entertained our friends.

Those were "big talk" days. We planned to buy silverware and Jim brought home samples from the jeweler in Mickey Cohen's building. One had to buy from some one and the shop was handy to Jim's.

I lived in a whirl, bounded on one side by diapers and on the other by Jim's complacent smile. Until, during that long summer of 1949, my happiness was pricked by one headline after another and life became one long heartache. Only once during that summer did I have a flare of hope. After months of not attending church, Jim suggested, "Let's go to church tonight."

Now I realize it was bravado on Jim's part. He was going to prove to his friends that he had done nothing of which he was ashamed and could attend church if he were in the mood. But ever the optimist I changed into my beige suit, and we left Madeline at my parents'.

When we reached the South Hollywood Presbyterian Church, some of his closer friends were as pleasant as ever but all too many of the members looked askance at Jim. Their unfriendly attitude discouraged me anew. If the Christians did not welcome him to church, how would he ever be convinced that he should change his ways and associates? What would ever get beneath the surface to the Jim Vaus who needed God? And there matters stood that late summer of '49.

CHAPTER SEVEN

In the Big Tent

They called my husband a gangster. Was he? There will always be a difference of opinion if he were or not. Mickey Cohen expressed his opinion on the subject. *The Los Angeles Daily News* June 13, 1949, ran a page interview with Mickey Cohen, including pictures of Cohen, his wife, LaVonne and his home. In it Cohen said:

"Jimmy (J. Arthur Vaus) the guy who made those recordings has done lots of work for me. He put in $3000 worth of radar and electronics stuff at my house."

Vaus had never mentioned a word about the recordings to him, said Cohen, but after Jackson began to press him for the records, he went to Vaus.

"I always thought of Jackson and his boss, Wellpott, as nice fellows," Mickey said, "and I told this to Vaus. But he don't see it that way. He told me them coppers was no good."

Yes, Jim worked for Mickey Cohen. But so did his laundry-men, his tailor, gardener and others. Merely working for a gambler does not make a man a gangster.

Was Jim a gangster because of the type of work he did for Cohen? Jim did wire-tapping, that is, he listened in on private telephone conversations. He also did this for the police department, for politicians, for motion picture stars who wanted to secure evidence for a divorce. Wire-tapping is legal in some states. His type of business alone could not have made him a gangster. Besides, he always insisted that his work for Cohen was legal, such as the time he put a radar screen around Cohen's house.

If Jim came close to being a gangster it was in his deals with some of the men he met through Cohen, such as Andy, the St. Louis racketeer. Jim was building a piece of equipment for this man which he was to take to St. Louis the early part of November. This, too, was "legal, perfectly legal, Honey." What worried me was that he would be leaving Los Angeles when I expected my second baby to be born.

About this time, much to my relief, the newspapers began leaving Jim, Cohen, et al, alone and concentrated on something vastly more interesting to me. Billy Graham and his evangelistic party, under the sponsorship of *Christ for Greater Los Angeles,* moved into a canvas cathedral at Washington and Hill, on the edge of the downtown shopping district.

REVIVAL HITS LOS ANGELES was the big headline those days. The campaign attracted such enormous crowds that accounts were printed in all the Los Angeles papers and in national magazines such as *Life* and *Time.* To quote one short item, an *Associated Press Wirephoto* of Billy Graham was printed in the *Los Angeles Herald-Express* with the caption:

A MODERN BILLY SUNDAY

At thirty, Evangelist Billy Graham is hailed by churchmen as a modern Billy Sunday. His six-week-old tent revival here is called the greatest in the history of Southern California. Converts number in the thousands.

The news was exciting and from the very beginning I wanted to hear Graham preach. I rejoiced at the thought of going to a service again always, there was the hope that God might touch Jim's heart. I prayed and prayed that He would. This might be the answer. I said to Jim, "Let's go hear Billy Graham. Your mother has heard him and says he is most interesting."

"Sure, we will, if we get time," he answered readily and that I knew was not a good sign. When Jim wasn't interested and did not intend to do a thing, he usually sloughed if off by being too agreeable, and never actually doing it.

The weeks went by. There was rumor after rumor that the campaign would close and then it would be extended another week. My hopes rode an elevator with every rumor. Meanwhile, I grew bigger and more uncomfortable as the date for our baby's birth grew closer.

Sunday, November 6 was a hot, sticky day in Los Angeles. Jim and I left not-quite-a-year-old Madeline with my parents and from then on, the day seemed part of an overall plan. Jim's uncle, Winfield Vaus, had unexpectedly died. About eleven o'clock we drove over to the Utter-McKinley mortuary to see him. Jim stood at the coffin, looking down at his uncle's body. I could see that he was touched. His uncle's death gave Jim a feeling of how suddenly one can be cut off. It hits a person to see their own lying cold and stiff. Who knows, maybe, you will be next!

It was a subdued Jim who walked out to the car with me and because it was so hot, we decided to go to a motion picture theatre which would be air-conditioned. We went to see *Pinky*. Again, Jim was hit in his weak spot. This picture was about a girl who pretended to be something she was not, just as Jim was bluffing about being a flourishing church member, the upright son of a minister and as good as the next fellow.

When we came out of the theatre, we drove toward the

beach, but even there, it was a cloudy, sticky day, so we started back toward town. I don't remember where we ate, but we must have stopped some place. We went by Mickey Cohen's and a couple of other places but no one whom Jim wanted to see was in. It was almost as if some invisible force were driving him on and on.

We drove down Washington Boulevard. Both of us were feeling low, with an inner need, but we did not say anything to each other. But I understood Jim well enough to sense that he felt as low as I did. I think both of us, about the same time, realized that we were near the revival tent and that it was nearly time for the evening meeting. Jim said, "Honey, how'd you like to go to the Big Tent and see what this fellow Graham is like?"

"Anything you say, dear," I agreed, trying not to sound anxious. If Jim felt he was being high-pressured, he would balk. So I sat there, apparently only pleasantly interested, while Jim parked.

The tent, which seated 6280, was jammed. We found a couple of seats on the side, near the rear. When Jim tells the story he admits he sat there critical of everyone and everything but I enjoyed it all. I responded to the thrill of being again with those who were interested in the Lord.

Cliff Barrows, a tall young man, with jet-black wavy hair, led the singing. He moved the entire audience with a wave of his trombone. He and his pretty wife, Billie, sang "Oh, it's real." I agreed—oh, yes the love of Jesus which has sustained me during these past heart-breaking months is real. I had not deserved His love. I had not lived as fully for the Lord as I should. But His love was real.

Billy Graham began to preach. Six-feet-two, with a shock of blond wavy hair and burning blue eyes he captured the attention of everyone in the audience. Every facet of my being was riveted upon what he said of God's judgment and God's mercy. It was wonderful!

When he gave the altar call, I bowed my head, knowing, "This is for me," and I prayed, "for Jim, too, Lord, please."

Jim sat there, impassive, apparently unmoved and I trembled with fear lest he had not been touched. "Dear Lord, I cried, if this doesn't touch him, what will? What will?"

The crowd rose as a mass to sing, "Almost persuaded now to believe, almost persuaded Christ to receive." Again my heart cried, "Persuade Jim, Lord, persuade him."

A wiry man with sparse hair and a determined look on his thin face, whom we later learned was "Uncle" Billy Schofield, grabbed Jim by the arm. Jim glared at him. Schofield bowed his head to pray and when he raised his eyes, Jim muttered, "I'll go."

I followed Jim down the aisle almost blind with relief and joy. I would have followed Jim anywhere but here I was, following him to the altar. "Oh, dear God, be sure Jim means everything he says or does tonight. Don't let it be empty words just because he knows the words."

We walked by the platform into a smaller connecting prayer tent. There, men and women were kneeling in front of chairs, praying, some crying. With each one was a Christian, talking and praying. A young woman talked to me but I was too stirred to remember who she was, or what she said. I was more interested in what was happening to Jim.

Cliff Smith, then president of *Christ for Greater Los Angeles*, spotted Jim and came directly to us. He is a portly man, with a decisive manner and knew Jim's father. He talked straight to Jim, but Jim didn't hear or remember much of what was said. Jim, who so rarely shows his feelings, wept. And each tear held a rainbow of promise to me. Something had got beneath that ever-smiling "I'll get by" surface.

He prayed, as he later admitted, "Lord, I mean business with You but You've got to mean business with Jim Vaus, for the road ahead is going to be a rough one. It's going to be almost impossible to straighten out this bewildered, tangled life of mine. But if You'll straighten it out, I'll turn it over to You—all of it."

At that moment I did not even know of the many wrongs Jim would have to straighten out. I only thought that if he were right with God, we would go to church and we would read the Bible. And naturally, that he would quit associating with Mickey Cohen and that gang, and stop being in the papers. But I had no idea how far-reaching Jim's decision would be.

When Jim finished praying, Cliff Smith introduced us to Billy Graham and his wife, Ruth, and to Cliff Barrows and his wife. I was happy to meet them and it seemed as if from that moment on, everything began clicking.

They warmly congratulated Jim on his step, and we moved down the aisle, onto the sidewalk. A reporter hurried up to us and said, "Hey, Vaus, you've had your picture in the paper for everything else, how about letting us shoot a couple more and tell us what happened tonight?"

Jim started to say no; then he paused, let the man take the picture and told them that he had gone forward to accept Christ as his personal Saviour. As we walked away, Jim remarked, "Well, that picture in the paper will let a lot of people know what is up and it will really change things."

The next day, the newspaper announced:

WIRE-TAPPER VAUS HITS SAWDUST TRAIL

That night, however, I was concerned only with the effect of Jim's decision upon our personal life and our families. We went to my parents' to pick up Madeline and I told mother, "Jim went forward at the Graham meeting."

"I knew Jim would," she whispered, squeezing my arm. Mother-like, she had completely ignored the fact that her angel-child had also felt the need of going forward.

When Jim and I reached home, I was tired but happy. I put Madeline in her crib and noticed that Jim seemed more disturbed than I thought he should be. While I was undressing he began, "Honey, you saw me make a decision tonight. You know I'm a changed man."

I nodded. Oh, I hoped, I hoped he was!

"Honey, you know some of my business dealings haven't been as straight as they should be."

I frowned. I supposed not. A man who was not right with God would not be too ethical. And I knew he was mixed up with a tricky lot, but always he had insisted that anything he did was "legal." He couldn't have done anything too bad. I crawled into bed and waited for him to continue.

"You know that little gadget in the garage."

Again I nodded. How often in the pleasant summer evenings I had sat on a garden chair in the entrance of the garage and watched him work. He had explained that he was making a piece of equipment for "some of the boys." It made a fascinating clicking sound and while I enjoyed being with him when he worked, I did not understand too much of what he was making.

"That was to help a mob in St. Louis beat the races. It's a piece of equipment we were planning to plug in on the Continental Wire Service. It would insert a delay so the teletype-writers on that line would not receive the messages until a minute and a half after we did. Meanwhile, we'd know who won the race and place our bets."

"Oh."

"But I won't go through with it now."

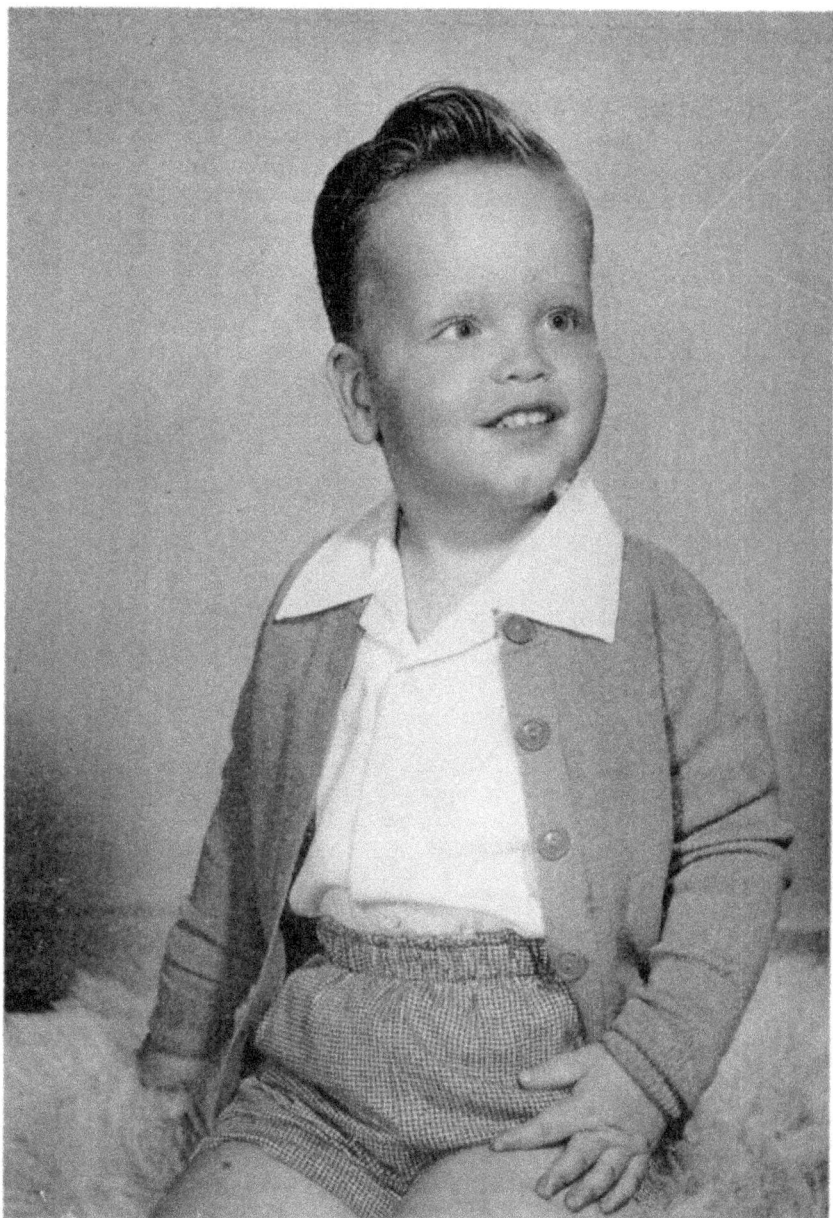

Dennis Craig

"Good." Yes, that was what his decision meant. No more associating with these queer characters.

"The boys won't like it."

"So what?"

He gave me a pitying look as if I did not understand the implication of his decision. And I didn't. I was too tired to think it through. I drifted off to sleep and slept soundly.

In the morning I came slowly out of my haze to find that Jim had got the phone, with its long cord, and brought it to the bed. He called his father and told him, "Dad, I accepted Christ as my Saviour last night at the Graham meeting. I'm a changed man."

He phoned his sister Betty, repeating, "I'm a changed man." He phoned several friends, with the refrain, "I'm a changed man" lulling me into contented happiness. There would be peace and quiet in our home at last. How thankful I was that I had hung on!

Then, Jim put in a long distance call to St. Louis and I strained every nerve, listening to what he had to say. He was telling this man Andy that he wouldn't meet him because he was a changed man. I could tell from the look on Jim's face that his being a changed man meant nothing to Andy. He didn't understand all the Lord could do for a person. Jim seemed worried, but when he hung up, he only said, "It'll work out someway, Honey. The Lord will work it out."

The Lord! From now on, Jim and I had Someone to help us. We had breakfast and discussed still further the thrill of the night before and he told me a little more about the Andy deal. The idea of his being mixed up with a crooked racing syndicate was depressing and I was thankful the Lord had reached Jim in time.

After ten o'clock I had a sharp tearing pain and I knew, this was it! The baby was coming. But I wasn't going through all the performance I had last time. No dashing through town in an ambulance and waiting hours at the hospital. Besides, I wanted oh, so very much, to attend the Graham meeting that night. The pains were about thirty minutes apart. Jim saw me stiffen each time so I admitted them adding, "But it may be tomorrow before the baby arrives."

Just to be safe, I packed Madeline's diapers and her clothes so we could leave her with mother, and I packed the few things I would want at the hospital. By evening the pains were twenty minutes apart. We stopped on the way to eat, and then drove to my parents' home.

All the conversation was of the Graham meeting. We invited Helen to go with us. Helen is a blonde, with short, fluffy hair and that evening she wore a new cocoa brown coat with slopping lines and a toque with a small feature. I may be prejudiced but she looked smart and pretty to me.

At the Big Tent we found seats in almost the same spot as the night before, on the side, near the rear. I did enjoy the singing but I did not get too much out of the sermon. My pains came ten minutes apart. One would shoot through me, I'd stiffen and Jim on one side and Helen on the other would look concerned and mutter, "If you want to go, don't just sit there, say so."

The pains kept coming closer and closer until they were three minutes apart. I mumbled, "We'd better go." Right in the middle of Graham's sermon we hurried out of the tent, into the car. As we drove along Jim kept looking for a pay phone. When he found one he called my doctor who was definitely disturbed because I had waited so long.

We reached the Hollywood Presbyterian Hospital some time after nine and about eleven Dennis Craig was born. In two days plenty new had been added! With a new baby, my husband a new man, I faced a new future.

CHAPTER EIGHT

Going, Going, Gone!

It was during the four days I was in the hospital that I had time to really think about what had happened to us. From the beginning, the change in Jim was startling. In many ways. While I was in the delivery room—that is when a husband is under as great a strain as he probably ever is in life—Jim started to light a cigarette. He stared at it and tossed away both the cigarette and the pack. He was through smoking!

When Madeline had been born, Jim had hung around the hospital most of the time. With Denny I had a semi-private room with a phone and while Jim visited me sometimes, more often he phoned he was going to the morning prayer meeting, to a special afternoon meeting or the evening meeting at the Big Tent.

The hospital chaplain heard of Jim's conversion, came in to congratulate me and pray with me. My roommate introduced me to her husband with the flourish, "Alice's husband was converted at the Graham meetings." I missed Jim's not being with me, but I was thankful he was going to the meetings. After all, though I had prayed and prayed, my faith had been a slim strand that summer of '49.

Now Jim was changed and so was I. While it is true that that evening in the Big Tent I was more concerned with what was taking place in Jim's heart, it is also true that the

Lord touched my heart. Jim would never come ahead of the Lord again. Days when I compromised for Jim's sake were over. From now on, it had to be all the day, all the way, with the Lord.

What a delight it was to ride home, sitting, oh, so close to my new husband. Mother, with the two babies, was in the back seat. As Jim drove, he talked of the meetings, telling of giving his testimony; "What's happened to me is so real that it wasn't easy to talk about it. But I managed to say that my life hadn't been all it should be and that from now on I was living so all my ways would please the Lord."

I was weak when we reached home so Mother took charge of the babies. Jim and I sat in the living room. He told me, "Honey, I've a million things to make right. I've stolen equipment from the telephone company, Warner Brothers' Broadcasting Station, Bleitz Camera Company and lots of others."

As fast as he confessed his wrong doings, I tried to find excuses for him. He needed the equipment! He didn't realize how wrong were the things he had been doing. But Jim found no excuses for himself. Rather, he began making a list of the money he must pay back. He even wrote down an old Bible Institute debt of '39. I wondered if he would ever finish writing. When he totalled the amount he said, "It's over fifteen thousand dollars."

"But Jim!" I gasped. "Where will you ever get that much money?"

He stretched his long legs in front of him and looked up at the ceiling. "Honey, I don't know. Believe me, I don't. But I do know I'm going all the way with the Lord and these are things I have to make right. I'll shut down my business, return tons of equipment that I swiped and sell the rest to raise some money. I'll do everything I can and the Lord will provide the rest."

I nodded. We did have a little money in the bank but Jim wasn't the saving kind. It wasn't that I didn't trust the Lord. I did. But $15,000 is a lot of money to pay back. Especially when your husband has no work, and you have two babies, one not even a year old and the other less than a week old.

We didn't discuss matters any more at that time. I was so weak I had to take my shocks in small doses. But at twilight I was sitting in the patio. It was a dreamy sort of a place, with a barbecue, and in the center, a large walnut tree. Jim had raked the leaves and was burning them.

My mind drifted back to some of the many things which had bothered me. Now I was married to a changed man perhaps I could learn the truth. I said, "Honey, do you remember the night someone tried to break into your car over at my folks, but you made it look worse? Why did you?"

He tossed some dry leaves into the fire. The flame burnt a bright orange and the leaves crackled. He stood under the tree, looking down at me. "Honey, I had to make it look as if those recordings had been stolen. Having them, put me in a spot and only if I could convince everyone concerned that I didn't have them would I be safe."

"But you did have the recordings. You buried them the time Burns came out here to watch them."

"I buried some recordings but actually they weren't the ones that the D.A.'s office wanted. That was why I buried them, so they could not play them and find out they were fake."

"But, Honey, why were you so afraid? I don't understand."

"I don't suppose you do. The police department was threatening to put me in jail if I didn't give them the records and Cohen and his friends were having an equal fit for fear I would. They had me as near sweating as I ever come."

"But where were the real recordings?" I persisted, ferreting out the mystery.

"That's the funny part of it and I couldn't get anyone to believe me. I told the truth to Rummel and he said I was handing him a line. I told Sharp and Corsini and they pooh-poohed me. But I had had those recordings hanging around the shop for months and played them as a gag to different friends. And sometime when I sold some equipment I inadvertently sold those spools too, and I've no idea to whom."

"Oh, no!" So it had all been much ado about nothing!

"The papers made the biggest fuss about them, but what was more important were things like some of the equipment I have in the garage, which isn't honestly mine."

Anxious, I bent forward and asked, "To whom does it belong?"

"The telephone company. I'm going to take it back to them. The phone company has been trying to trace me for months because of my wire-tapping. They certainly will be hopping mad when I admit I've also been acquiring their equipment without their consent. And Honey—" His face grew pale and drawn. "I'm going to admit I committed perjury in the Jackson case. Suppose they arrest me and send me to prison?"

I was too shocked to answer. I sat there, my hands clasped together and stared at the home that I had thought was going to be so wonderful now Jim was a Christian. Here he was, telling me it might all be swept away. If ever a woman needed her husband, it was I. But I wasn't thinking of myself, but of Jim. Jim wearing a rough blue uniform. Jim eating that starchy, gummy food. Jim behind bars!

"Honey, suppose—" he prompted.

"If God allows it, then it would be all right," I answered and I really meant it. But my heart cried, "Lord, don't take Jim away from me. You answered my prayer and kept Jim for me until I was old enough to marry him. Now I have him, dear God, please let me keep him."

As I look back, the exact sequence of events blurred, but I know that each day brought a fresh need to trust the Lord. There was the day he went to the telephone company and I knew they could prefer Grand Theft charges but Claude Peters, the telephone official, was so convinced that Jim was a changed man that he even offered him a job. There was the day when Andy and his hoodlums came to the house to demand that Jim string along with them in their racket. But Jim convinced even them that he was a changed man and they left him alone. There were other days when he took the risk of admitting other wrongs and making them right. And the day he went to court to admit he had committed perjury. All these were days to walk by faith!

He soon closed his shop and announced, "I'm through with electronics. It has brought me nothing but grief."

"But Honey, maybe you could use your knowledge for the Lord."

"How?" he demanded.

I couldn't tell him how so we dropped the subject. One day he brought home a tape recording of his testimony at the Graham tent. A friend had taken it for me. It was a thrill to hear it. This was a new kind of wire-recording for Jim Vaus and it deepened my conviction that the Lord would yet use Jim's knowledge of electronics.

Each day we seemed to have less and less money. We bought only the food we actually had to have. When I could I went to the meeting and Jim went to all of them. The day came, when, as he left, he remarked, "Honey, I've only enough gas to get to town. I'll leave the car on the parking lot and tell the finance company to come get it."

"But how will you get home?"

"Hitch-hike."

I could not picture my proud Jim using his thumb to hail a ride but I didn't say anything. Instead, off and on, during the evening, I prayed. And sure enough, just a little later than his usual time, a car drove up and out stepped Jim. He came into the house, kissed me and handed me a box. "For Denny. From Margaret McCraw of the Country Church of Hollywood."

"Let me see." Excited, I opened the box and it was filled with darling knitted garments for Denny and Madeline. Things which I did not have for the children. It was a delight to receive them. It was the first time a stranger had ever given me anything for nothing. But I have learned that Christians can be almost off-handed in their giving when they want to help someone.

Then he showed me two five dollar bills. He explained, "Billy Schofield got me the ride and pushed this in my breast pocket, and Alfred Dixon, who drove me home, put this bill in my Bible, lying on the seat between us. I'm not going to take the money. Why, they're hard working men. I've squandered my share and I'm not going to take from them."

My dear big-shot Jim, how it hurts his pride to take from others! I reminded, "You said you'd trust the Lord to provide."

"But this way?"

"You have to let the Lord choose the way. Besides Jim, maybe this is God's way of making you humble."

We prayed and he not only kept the money but sincerely thanked the Lord for it.

Jim now had either to take the bus into Los Angeles or to hitch-hike. He never did reach the place where he could use his thumb with ease but he used to stand at the bus stop and hope and hope until someone came along and offered him a ride. After he found he could use his contact with a stranger as an opportunity to testify for the Lord, he didn't mind so much.

Our losses didn't stop with the car. Next whatever of the furniture we could spare we sold to pay debt and pay for food.

Of course, Mother had to go home. She had her family to look after. I had my hands full with the two babies and also found that keeping house on a limited budget was far more difficult than when I was able to spend right and left. It meant more thought and more work. We looked around for someone to help me.

Shortly before Jim had been converted, Alyce Brooks had gone forward at the October 15 Billy Graham meeting. She was a slender capable young woman who worked as secretary for the Western Harness Racing Ass'n at Hollywood Park. They had charge of the sulky races where gambling for high stakes was involved; so Alyce felt impelled to quit.

She and Jim both attended the smaller testimony and prayer meetings in the prayer tent in the afternoons. One day she told her story. Afterwards she and Jim began talking, drawn together by their mutual conversion and the change in their lives.

Alyce, with her teen-age daughter, Virginia, lived in a

small house, and now Alyce had no work, each day, she was getting more and more broke.

One morning, after devotions—Jim always seemed to have his best ideas after devotions—he phoned Alyce and asked her if she didn't want to come live with us. We could combine our little and with the Lord's help, each one of us would be a little less broke.

She and her daughter moved in with us the twelfth of December and once more I was thrilled by the Christian spirit which prompted one to share. She was of infinite help, staying with the babies, pressing Jim's suits. Also, she was a help spiritually. I remember one night when Jim phoned he had neither car fare nor a way to get home. She got out of bed and prayed with me. In about an hour, in walked Jim. A preacher friend had driven by where Jim was waiting and brought him home.

Two nights before Christmas Jim and I went shopping. It was the first time I had ever gone any place with Jim on the bus. When we came back, with our arms full of packages, we had to walk several blocks in the crisp night air. It was fun. We divided Christmas Day between the two parents' homes. New Year's he was away, speaking at *Youth For Christ* in San Francisco.

Living as we were, from day to day, we were unable to make the payments on our home. In fact, Jim said, "What right have I to own so big a house when I owe so much?"

I should have been amazed when Jim said that but by this time nothing he said surprised me. It did not sound natural for Jim Vaus to think he ought to pay his debts before he bought something for himself but that was the attitude of the new Jim.

He phoned Mr. F. B. Johnson and told him we couldn't meet our payments. He gave us a reasonable amount of time in which to move. We considered the ways and means of getting another place to live. We couldn't go live with my parents. They did not have the room. There was plenty of room in the Vaus home but we did not tell them. We kept our troubles to ourselves. To go back home, broke, meant that the Lord could not take care of us and we felt that He would.

Jim phoned his new friends to have them try to locate a place to live. If we could even find a place we would trust the Lord to provide the rent but it was during the housing shortage and there were no vacancies. We had faith that the Lord would provide, only, by now, we knew the Lord did not do things ahead of time so we did not have to worry, but only when the right time came.

Meanwhile it was *Youth For Christ* which had been arranging for Jim to give his testimony at different meetings. One day, Helen Boyer, the secretary phoned and said, "Jim, I noticed you had no commitments for January so I told a little church in Gardena you'd hold two weeks of meetings for them."

"I couldn't speak for two nights, let alone two weeks," he objected.

When he told me he had refused, I was sorry. I recalled the evening we had gone to that church. It was such a warm little place. It had been a men's dinner. The wives had cooked it and I sat in the kitchen with them, and later, after the dishes were washed, we went in and listened to Jim. But the idea of preaching for two weeks floored him. At that time, he had no idea what he was going to do, but he certainly had no thought of becoming a minister or an evangelist. Mostly, he was concentrating upon clearing up the mess in his life.

But the Lord would not let Jim forget the Gardena invitation. One morning, after our family devotions, he rose from the table, crossed the room, picked up the phone and dialed *Youth For Christ.* While the number was ringing, he glanced at me and said, "Helen is so efficient I'm sure she has cancelled those meetings, but if, by any chance, she hasn't, I'll take them."

Helen had not cancelled the meetings!

So Jim Vaus became a preacher. He had attended the Bible Institute of Los Angeles and he had heard his father preach since he was a boy but when it came to actually giving a message, he had to dig. Each day he would sweat over his sermon. He objected, "I can't do it. I don't know what to say."

"Who is giving this message, you or the Lord?" I reminded him.

He relaxed and went back to his praying and studying. It was refreshing to see Jim, not depending upon Jim Vaus, but upon the Lord.

Among the many wonderful things which happened to us at this time was the friendship of Dawson Trotman. He is the head of *The Navigators,* an organization which specializes in reaching men in the armed forces for Christ as well as doing follow-up work for other organizations. Trotman assigned one of his men to drive Jim to the meeting each night.

The days continued to trickle by like sand running through an over-sized hourglass. The day Mr. Johnson had set for us to be out of the house was only two days away!

On Sunday morning Jim took a two-hour bus ride to a church and when he arrived, he learned he had come the wrong Sunday. As he rode home, he reviewed the Navigator's memory course of Bible verses which he had been studying.

When he came in the house, Alyce, Virginia and I were

eating dinner. Jim's face was beaming. He almost shouted, "Honey, I know the Lord will provide a house for us. Look," and he read, " 'Hitherto have ye asked nothing in My Name, ask and ye shall receive that your joy may be full' (John 16: 24). For years I knew about Jesus but I didn't ask anything in His name but now I've asked for a house in His name."

That afternoon Alyce was to stay home with the babies while I went to the meeting with Jim. I dressed in some of the finery of our former high days. Jim and I had had matching custom made suits and that day I wore mine with red shoes and accessories.

The evangelist, Rev. Stevens, sent a couple of young men to drive us to the meeting. After Jim spoke, Rev. Steven announced, "We won't take an offering today. Instead, as you go out, I want each one of you to shake Jim's hand and leave something in it, or slip something in his pocket."

Jim and I stood at the back door and shook hands with what seemed like two hundred and fifty people. Each one put a coin or a bill in our hand, or in our pocket, and that, I know, took the last vestige of false pride out of Jim.

Many people spoke to him that day so I did not especially notice when Pat Thornbury talked to him. Once we were in the car Jim grinned his positively largest variety of grin and said, "Honey, we've a home."

"We've what?"

"Pat Thornbury said he just finished building a new house and that while I gave the message the Lord told him to let us have the house and also spoke to Mrs. Thornbury. And when a woman is willing to give up a home, it has to be the Lord."

The last tie with the old life was broken. The electronics business, the car, the furniture, the house was gone. Now, everything we had was the Lord's provision.

CHAPTER NINE

So This is the New Life

The change in my life was complete. I had ceased to be a woman in a home with a degree of luxury, waiting, night after night, for my husband to leave his unsavory companions and come home. I had become a woman living in a rented home in Whittier, with two babies, knowing my husband would not be home. He had become an evangelist and was in some strange city, long miles from me.

Alyce and her daughter, Virginia, had had to move back to Los Angeles. Alyce went to work as secretary for *Christ for Greater Los Angeles.* I had no car so it was no longer possible to leave Madeline and Denny even with my willing mother. I was tied to the house and babies. It was an attractive home and the babies were dears, but there was no Jim. Not even at four in the morning!

When Jim began giving his testimony and then preaching I suppose that secretly I had hoped he would take a church and I would settle down to be a minister's wife. During the week, Jim and I could visit the sick. On Saturday Jim would be in his study, preparing his sermon, while I cleaned house. On Sunday, I would sit in a pew while Jim preached. All my dreams had a togetherness.

Instead, each evening at twilight I watched the cars drive up the street. Husbands got out of them to go into *other* homes. Or men who rode the bus, with quickness in their step, walked down the block to *other* homes. No husband came to my house. During the evening, about two houses down the street, a couple worked in their garden. Nostalgia for Jim flooded me.

Of course I wanted him to be a Christian. He had to be, but I had not expected that being one would take him so completely from me. As the waves of self-pity engulfed me I recognized that they were wrong and I fought them. I reminded myself that I had what I wanted. But my erring heart complained, "You want Jim, too, don't you?"

One evening when I had dinner at the Navigator's home, Dawson Trotman and I discussed my problem. His lean face looked concerned as he said, "Alice, you have no idea the number of wives who hinder their husband's Christian service by their self-pity. It weighs a man down until he doesn't feel free to go where the Lord would have him go. Eventually, some of these men compromise to please their wives, taking the Lord's second best."

"I couldn't do that to Jim," I knew.

"Let me give you a verse, Alice. God's Word says, 'There is no man that hath left house, or parents, or brethren, or wife or children for the kingdom of God's sake, who shall not receive manifold more in this present time and in the world to come life everlasting' (Luke 18:29,30)."

I hugged that verse close to my heart during the long, hot summer. I stranded my self-pity. Each one of us could be sorry for ourselves on some score. I would not let it eat, like acid, into my life. When Jim and I did snatch a few days together, they were more precious than ever. Then, though we were in different states, the same idea came to both of us. It was as if the Lord were showing us how we could be together more. We should buy a trailer and the babies and I could travel with Jim.

About ten months after Jim's decision for Christ, in September, 1950, we returned the home to Pat Thornbury and through J. Paul Getty, one of Jim's former clients, we bought a *Spartan* trailer. It seemed impossible that this shiny thirty-three feet of space could hold every essential for a home but I found it even more convenient than a house. We even had a phone in the car so that anyone who knew what state we were in could reach us.

We started for Boston where Jim was to hold meetings. By the time we reached Springfield, Missouri, we found that we could not get to Boston by the specified date. We simply could not make the time with the trailer that we had hoped to. So, once more, Jim parked me while he went to hold his campaign.

This time he left me in a trailer camp in a town where I did not know a soul. Naturally, I am shy and diffident. For years I had clung to Jim, letting him make the friends, arrange contacts, run our lives. Now if anything were to be done, I had to do it. I could stay quietly with my babies and brood, or I could pray and let the Lord draw me out. I chose the latter.

In the wash house I found myself talking to Jean Halda-man. She had two children eight and twelve. Her husband had been recently converted and was studying at the nearby Baptist college. When I told her who Jim was, and where he was, she was most interested in him. She soon realized how completely stranded I was and suggested, "Let me teach you to drive."

I gulped. But I knew that the Lord was going to teach me to do many things if I were to live in His Spirit. Therefore, on rutty country roads, with my heart in my throat, I learned to drive.

In due time, Jim flew back to me. I said good-by to

Steven Timothy

Jean and once more snuggled down besides Jim, letting him drive, letting him make the decisions. I was back to being the contented wife.

We drove south to Atlanta, where Jim worked on the public address system for the Graham meetings. Then, we went to Jim's meetings in the Philadelphia area. It was about that time that Jim first talked of using scientific equipment as a medium of contact with high school young people, giving platform demonstrations of new developments in the field of chemistry, physics and electronics.

I could see how acceptable this would be for high school assemblies, but I wondered how well it could be used in evangelistic meetings.

A couple of nights later he stood on the platform in front of a huge crowd of people, and holding in his hand two ten dollar bills, he announced. "After the ushers have given these to any two men in the audience I will come back in and tell you who has the ten dollar bills, what pocket they have them in, and perhaps tell you something about the men who received the money."

Jim went behind the stage where he could not see what was happening. The ushers gave out the bills. One man hid a bill in his shoe, the other in the cuff of his trousers. Jim came out and in an amazingly short time he had located the bills. Later he drew from his illustration in a message he had brought on, "You Cannot Hide From God."

What Jim did not explain was how he had found the bills. I dare not tell you how he did it for you may one day be the victim in a similar audience. Simple when one knows how, and some day maybe many of the ways of God, which seem so mysterious, will seem as simple.

It was in Philadelphia that Jim injured his eyes in the use of some of his equipment. That night when he went to bed, his eyes burned. He tossed. He moaned. He turned. He groaned. About three in the morning, desperate, he asked, "Alice, do you think you can really drive? Could you get me to a hospital?"

Springfield was miles behind me. Could I remember all that Jean had taught me? I prayed and put on a brave front. "Of course I can drive."

Jim could not even open his eyes. I had to lead him to the car and drive in that bewildering strange town. He was so nervous that it seemed to him that everything I did was wrong. But I did get him to the hospital, and the doctor gave him some salve which helped him. My Springfield experience had come into good use!

We went to the Cleveland area for more meetings and more cold weather. Then headed toward Chicago. I had better explain, the planning of an evangelist's itinerary is far more complicated than people realize. Ministers or committees write, asking him to hold meetings. Jim has to figure out where he will be when to work in as many meetings as possible, with as little traveling, and no back-tracking, between meetings. It requires a great deal of prayer and managing to get word back and forth, lining up meetings.

In Chicago, the children and I again lived in a trailer park. I have lived in various trailer parks all over the United States and find that in them, each little group lives its own life. In the main, no one is interested in a lonely wife with two small children. In each camp my needs were the same and the Lord was the same Lord with His sustaining power.

My uncle gave my sister Helen money to fly to Chicago and she was to travel back to the coast with us. How I looked forward to having Helen's company! I met her at the airport early in the morning. In the afternoon Jim and I showed her some of the sights of Chicago and in the evening while Jim went to his meeting, Helen and I talked about the hundred and three little things which happened to our families while I was on my trailer trek.

When Jim got back from the meeting in Bloomington, the weather was growing increasingly worse. It sleeted and snowed in turns. Jim felt that we should travel as far as we could that night, and that it was safe as long as there was no ice on the road. I put Denny to sleep on the floor and Madeline on the back seat. Helen and I sat in front beside Jim.

We drove through the murky streets of Chicago, out of the city, until we came to a bridge. We started across it and swish—that awful helpless feeling of skidding. The trailer swung completely around, whirling the car with it and knocking us into a car coming from the other direction.

Moisture had risen from the river and formed a thin coating of ice on the bridge. The children slept through it, Helen was petrified and I—well, none of us were hurt and that was what counted.

Jim called the police on the car phone, and we waited in the penetrating cold. The bridge had tall sides so other cars could not see the wreck. Fortunately Jim had some flares with him. He lit one to warn oncoming drivers but even so a couple of cars came to a sliding stop, not understanding the meaning of the flares.

When the cold and dark had seemingly sapped the last bit of strength, the cops came, and they got in touch with a garage. A tow truck towed us back to the same trailer camp from which we had started!

The next day we waited while the car was repaired. Helen marveled that we were all safe and sound despite the accident. She kept referring to Jim's habit of praying before we started. She said over and over again, "I'm so glad you prayed last night before you started."

[83]

Evening came and we began our journey again. Though we did not go far, we did get safely over the bridge. But the accident had proved to us still further that the trailer was not going to work out as we had hoped. In it, Jim could not make the time he had to make and it was not safe to drive during possible icy weather.

From Oklahoma City, Helen flew home and Jim drove me as far South as he could. Then he went to Great Falls, Montana, leaving me in Roswell, New Mexico. I was there over two weeks and truly *no one* spoke to me. I read and reread the verse, "I have learned, in whatsoever state I am, therewith to be content" (Phil. 4:11). To Paul, *state* meant condition but to me, it meant the state of Missouri, of Pennsylvania, of Massachusetts, of Illinois, of New Mexico, or whatever state, therein to be content.

I understand how Sarah felt when Abraham became a pilgrim and stranger from the land of Ur. No doubt Sarah knew a stall in the market place where she found the plumpest dates. She knew a weaver who made cloth exactly the right thickness. But Abraham was called of God.

No longer could she go to the river and wash clothes with her friends. Each day all familiarity of sameness was stripped from her anew and she started out again. She met the needs of her family in strange bazaars where she hoped she was not over-charged. She rode beside her husband on his great adventure.

Sarah rode a camel, I in a trailer, but I felt a kinship with her and the countless women who have followed a husband called of God. The greatness of God is that as He leads a man with a drive and verve to win souls; He also comforts the heart of the woman who follows.

It was in those cities all over the United States where I waited for Jim that I learned to walk with the Lord. I

had time to read my Bible as I should, to meditate on the promises and find my contentment in Him. I learned to say, "All my springs are in thee" (Ps. 87:7).

When Jim picked me up in Roswell, we hoped to be home for Christmas. The first day on the road we found we could not make any time. The car simply would not make the hills. December 22, we spent the day in an oily garage. The children played in the back seat while the men worked on the car. The mechanic put one new part after another into the car until the bill was a hundred dollars. Still, it would not run as it should. The mechanic scratched his head and frowned, "Let's try new spark plugs."

"Don't you remember," Jim reminded. "When I first came in, I said it might be spark plugs and you said it couldn't be."

The mechanic glared at Jim, tried new spark plugs and that was what had been wrong all the time! By now we had nearly everything new in the car so we stepped along, arriving in front of Vaus home sometime during the night. We slept in the trailer until the next morning when Mr. Vaus came out and found us. Christmas, divided among our two families, was a joyous occasion.

In January Jim started out again. I did not attempt to go with him. Instead the trailer was parked in the backyard of the Wendt's home in San Fernando Valley. You may remember that Lester Wendt is a minister. At the time Betty worked as a nurse in an office. While I was alone during the day, in the evening it was cozy to sit in her living room. She knitted and I learned about being a minister's wife.

Had I wildly dreamed that a minister had time to be with his wife! A minister has a full time job of laying down his life for the brethren. When someone dies, he is called to comfort the widow. Rightly so. When someone is ill, the minister is called to pray. Rightly so. When a divorce is considered, a boy is wayward, no matter what the problem, the minister is called. Rightly so. God has called him to help others but if a girl is looking for constant companionship she will find it with a minister serving his congregation.

I have an idea that there isn't any job for a man where a wife sees as much as she wants of the one she loves. This is the Lord's design. If a wife were to find all her needs satisfied by a husband, she would stop there, taking second best, instead of going on to know the Lord fully.

In June, Jim and I were to leave again in the trailer. This time, to go North. By now, he was carrying a ton of electronic equipment, necessitating a station wagon which one of the Navigators, Don Hardy, drove and with him rode Ken Nanfelt.

When I had everything ready, I said to Jim, "We're all packed."

"That's what you think." He gave his most tantalizing smile. What was coming now? It was books. Rafts of books. Piles of books. Stacks of books. Jim had given the Navigators the right to the story of his conversion and we sold the book, the profits going to them. So there I was with *Why I Quit Syndicated Crime* to the right of me, to the left of me. I stepped over them. I reached over them. Every nook and cranny of the trailer was filled with books. My only break was that as we went from town to town, Jim sold some of them. Gradually, but all too gradually, there was room again in the trailer.

When Jim spoke in Molalla, he asked me to step to the microphone, introduced me and urged, "Say something, Honey."

I managed to gasp, "Hello," and that was the limit of my speaking in public.

It was in a city-wide campaign in Yakima, Washington, that I first heard Jim's message, "Heaven is Real." This campaign was backed by the greater number of churches in the Yakima area. In fact, I believe that people from more than seventy-five different churches gave their support.

I could see how very well the use of this great array of scientific equipment could drive home a point, never to be forgotten. So many folks say they will not believe anything they cannot see, or least feel or hear. Jim shows them how inadequate are the human senses. He proves they cannot see well at all, nor can they hear, nor have they any sense of feeling. In fact, by the time he finishes he shows that the average person can't even think clearly. But best of all, I like the way he uses the Bible to clearly establish the facts. He never tries to prove the Bible with scientific gadgets, but proves how superior the authority of the Bible is to the textbooks of Science. This message on heaven sent me away feeling more certain in my heart than ever that the day of the LORD'S return is near at hand, and most certainly, heaven is real!

It was in Yakima that Jim agreed that I would speak at a special afternoon meeting for ladies only. Not me! I remembered too vividly how I had quaked in Molalla.

But yes, it was announced. I knew an entire week ahead and, though I found a number of verses in the Bible suitable for the occasion, none of them comforted me. I could not speak in public. I do very well with one person, but from a banquet on, I am in a panic. I knew that whatever was done the Lord would have to do, and I didn't see how He could do much with as little in me with which to work.

It was a warm day when we gathered in the special building at the Yakima Fair Grounds, with a sea of over five hundred women's faces staring at me. Jim was relaxed. Why not? He didn't have to speak. The meeting began. My nerves twisted into one solid ball in the pit of my stomach. Herb Jauchin, who was arranging the meetings, passed me a slip of paper. I unfolded it and read, "And when he putteth forth his own sheep, he goeth before them" (John 10:4). That was exactly what I needed!

I had made Jim promise that he would stand beside me the entire time I spoke, but when I began, Jim saw that the Lord had given me peace, so he sat down. Briefly, I said:

"As I have travelled across the United States, in strange town after strange town, I have learned that if a Christian woman is to be happy, she must put her time alone with the Lord first. Even ahead of her husband and her children. Only from the Lord will she receive strength for the day and its problems. The days that I neglected being alone with the Lord, everything seemed to go wrong. But when I took time for my devotions there was such a difference in the day. I have learned to ask the Lord to help me with everything, even things which seem simple to others, but are important to me, such as getting the wash done.

"If a woman has time alone each day with the Lord, no matter how weak she may be, she will learn that the Lord keeps His promise, 'My grace is sufficient for thee; for my strength is made perfect in weakness' (II Cor. 12:9)."

The trek began again. We went to Seattle where I settled down in a trailer park and waited while Jim flew to Alaska for meetings. It was one more city in which I learned to rely solely upon the Lord. Again I saw people live their individual lives with scarcely a word for another. It surprised me that in trailer parks where they must all be strangers, suffering the same loneliness that so few were friendly.

Jim came back and we started down the coast, stopping for a few meetings. It was September and I had spent a year in the trailer. I was expecting either Stephen Timothy or Joanna Christine. We felt we needed more than a trailer for our growing family and prayed, "Where now, Lord?"

CHAPTER TEN

Bright Tomorrow

As Jim and I made our way down the coast, an idea began to form in our minds. For some months Jim's parents had been trying to sell the old homestead. It was a large house and now that the children were grown, there was more room and work than was necessary for the two of them. In contrast, here were Jim and I with a growing family who needed room.

Jim wrote his parents our proposition. When we reached Los Angeles we drove by his father's church to pick him up. He was always so pleased to see us! We went to the house, discussed buying it and within an hour—the deal was settled. That it was the Lord's will for us was confirmed when, the next day, a man offered to buy the house for cash.

We enjoy living in the old home. As we can afford it, we are repapering, buying new curtains and doing all the things which a woman enjoys doing to a house.

My bright tomorrow has come. I look back and see how the Lord prepared me for today. I shrank from the developing process but now am thankful for it. It took that year on the road to prepare me to manage the house and govern the children with Jim away.

Among the many things I do for Jim is read his mail. What an insight into the human heart is the mail of an evangelist! Men ask point blank if it is possible to live a straight life for Christ. Women who battle with doubt write for a panacea. The answer is the giving of the will, a hundred times a day, if necessary, to the Lord. Teen-age boys, tempted to run with the gang respond to someone who will show them a better way. Teen-age girls offer their hero worship.

One of them recently wrote, asking for Jim's picture. She was writing a theme for high school on the subject "My Great American." She reminded me of my girlhood days when I had written a theme about Jim, his army record and church attendance. I received one of the best grades I ever made for it.

When Jim is home how different life is from the old days! He is perfectly content to stay home. Perhaps that is the biggest change of all in Jim. In the vice-squad-Cohen days there were many times when Jim's love for me was casual. Now, well, love is always difficult to talk about but God can improve even the quality of a man's love.

Enough time has elapsed since November 1949 to reveal values in their true light. At the time, there were those who doubted Jim's wisdom in leaving "syndicated crime." A few days after Jim was converted he went to Cohen's home in Brentwood, one of the swankiest districts in Los Angeles. Jim always admired the Cohen home. It was surrounded by an acre of lawn, shrubs, citrus and avocado trees. The grass was tailored. There were always a couple of gardeners who scurried around to snip an extra leaf off the rose bushes in the formal gardens.

Jim often had dinner with the Cohens and knew the frequent ringing of the phone, of the doorbell. In those days, the Cohens were riding high and popular.

That time when Jim went there, he was shown into Cohen's den. It was a long room, running three-fourths of the length of the house. The furniture was rich cabinetwork, without a nail in it. There were huge brass lamps, flower pots, and ivy trailing gracefully off the mantle.

At one end of the room stood LaVonne, Dee David and wives of several men prominent in gangsterland. One of them called, "Jim, is it true that you've got religion?"

He walked quietly toward the women and answered, "You might call it that though I prefer to say I've found Christ. Anyway, something has happened to me and I have peace in my heart since I've settled things with God."

LaVonne glanced at Jim with a puzzled expression on her round face; then she turned away and stared out of the window with a far away look. She remarked, "I could use a little of that religion myself." Suddenly self-conscious, she gave a light, brittle laugh.

Mickey came in. Jim and he left the women and Jim told Cohen of his decision.

"There's a lot of people that won't like what you're doing," Mickey said. "They'll figure you're running out on them, taking the small end. But just remember this Jim, if the whole world turns against you, there's one little guy who thinks a lot of you for the decision you've made. Promise me one thing; that you'll never go back to your old way of life. Quit it for good."

Jim promised and it is well known that he has kept his promise.

Every opportunity thereafter he talked to Mickey about the Lord. He even arranged for Mickey to meet some of his Christian friends and have dinner with them. In the group were Dawson Trotman, Dick Hillis, former missionary to China and now in Formosa, Cohen and Sam Farkas.

Farkas was Cohen's body guard and was called "Big Sam." He is a husky fellow, good-looking in a brutish sort of a way. Naturally Jim, Trotman and Hillis steered the conversation around to the subject of the Lord.

Farkas stopped eating and reflected, "You guys is right. It's really the truth that there are no atheists in fox holes. I know. I saw plenty of action during the war and when I got in a pinch, I didn't stop to think if or if not there was a God. Plenty quick I prayed to Him. But you see how it is, I ain't in no fox hole now. I'm getting along all right without God."

This was as far as any of the gang would go. They figured they were smart and that Jim was the loser.

Time passed. Cohen was arrested for income tax evasion. Farkas headed up Cohen's business. In November 1951, Billy Graham and the members of his evangelistic party came to Hollywood and held meetings in the Bowl. Jim was in town part of the time and phoned, inviting LaVonne to hear Graham. She agreed to go and so Jim drove to the Brentwood home.

When he parked he was amazed at the change in the place. The trim green lawn had grown tall, withered and died. The formal garden was a mass of weeds.

Jim rang the bell and when a maid admitted him, the first thing he noticed was the resounding thud of his shoe on the bare floor. Gone were the plush carpets. Gone were the expensive furnishings. He went into the den where two years ago a group of monied women had laughed at his "getting religion." On a kitchen chair sat LaVonne Cohen. She glanced around sadly and remarked, "Looks a little different, doesn't it?"

"Yes," he nodded. The once well-to-do woman in her stripped mansion was pathetic.

"Remember the good times we used to have?"

"Do I!" A flood of memories, of delicious cursine, of thick steaks, of crisp salads, of gleaming silverware crowded into his mind.

"They're all gone. Remember how the phone use to ring?"

"Sure." That had been part of the game; the demanding tingle of the phone made a man feel important.

"It doesn't ring anymore. Remember how the doorbell used to ring? People wanting favors of Mickey?"

"Sure," Jim nodded again. The entourage surrounding Cohen, like courtiers about a king, had all been part of being a big-shot. The more people who asked favors of one, the bigger one felt he was.

"The doorbell doesn't ring anymore. The money is all gone and so are the friends." She stood up, a disconsolate droop to her shoulders.

She and Jim picked up Sam Farkas and went to the meeting in the Hollywood Bowl under the starry sky. Graham preached one of his usual forceful messages and many thronged to the altar. But Farkas and LaVonne sat still in the darkness.

After the people surged down the ramp, out of the bowl, Jim and LaVonne went to one of the small rooms behind the rostrum to talk to Graham. He spoke to her straight of her need of Christ. She agreed, "I'd be willing. I think Jim and you have something. But I can't, unless Mickey goes with me."

Reluctantly Jim took her to her empty home. Shortly afterwards she lost the home and moved into an apartment in Hollywood. Cohen was taken to McNeil Island Penitentiary. How completely the tables have turned! Jim had been in McNeil Island Penitentiary during his trouble in the army but he came out, to trust Christ as Saviour. Now, Cohen is in there.

Nor have things gone well for Mickey's pals. On January 26, 1952, the *Mirror* ran an article:

A complete investigation into an alleged attempt to murder Sam Farkas, former bodyguard of Mickey Cohen, was begun today by the 1952 grand jury as its first job.

Farkas told the jury Joseph Di Stefano, 36, an ex-convict from New York tried to shoot him in a Gardena oil field yesterday morning and when that failed, drove him to Hollywood to do the job right.

Farkas, who is 34 and lives at 1050 E. 99th St., said his life was saved by a traffic policeman who heard him shout for help at Hollywood and Cahuenga Blvds.

Di Stefano, who was booked on suspicion of murder, was to testify before the grand jury today.

Other witnesses to be called are the policeman who "saved" Farkas' life and Hollywood detectives.

Police said they went to the Gardena oil field yesterday afternoon and found prints of Di Stefano's crepe-soled shoes and an ejected 32 caliber shell. Di Stefano had an automatic pistol in his belt when he was arrested."

On March 17, the *Herald* reported that Sam Farkas "a member of Mickey Cohen's fast-dwindling old mob has been mysteriously missing for more than a month." Now that Farkas is in the equivalent of a fox hole I wonder if he is again calling on God, or if it is too late!

My heart goes out in sympathy to LaVonne Cohen and to all the other women in the world who are waiting for their husbands to make a step toward God. You simply can't wait for them. The verse which the Lord gave me when Jim was not a Christian not only said "be in subjection to your own husband" but also "that they may be gained by the behavior of their wives" (I Pet. 3:1).

It is up to the wife to be an example to her husband. Not a loud, talking example but a quiet, patient one. A

[95]

woman must be willing to follow God and trust Him to change her husband's life.

Each one of us as individuals must make our own choice. We must decide what is our answer to, "What think ye of Christ?" The answer should be that He is your Saviour because He said, "I am the Way, the Truth, and the Life" (John 14:6).

You have eternal life only as you believe that Jesus Christ is the unique Son of God, that He existed with God the Father before the beginning of time, came to earth and died for our sins according to the Scriptures, was buried and rose again according to the Scriptures.

The belief in the Lord Jesus Christ, which is total invasion of the heart and life by Christ, is of the heart, "for with the heart man believeth unto righteousness; and with the mouth confession is made unto salvation" (Rom. 10:10).

This belief will result in a life which is pleasing to God if you "observe to do according to all that is written therein." That is written in the Bible. When you walk according to God's Word, you can pray with confidence that your loved ones may also come to know the Lord Jesus Christ as Saviour.

This choice is yours. Have you invited Christ into your heart and life?

If you do not fully understand, write me and I will be most happy to send you a booklet on how to become a Christian and how to live for the Lord Jesus Christ.

Mrs. Jim Vaus
Post Office Box 62
Los Angeles 53, California

www.ingramcontent.com/pod-product-compliance
Lightning Source LLC
Chambersburg PA
CBHW051841040426
42447CB00006B/646